D1542645

An Ounce of Prevention

A Parent's Guide to Moral
and Spiritual Growth
of Children

An Ounce of Prevention

A Parent's Guide to Moral
and Spiritual Growth
of Children

Dr. Bruce Narramore
Psychologist

Illustrated by Diane Head

ZONDERVAN
PUBLISHING HOUSE

OF THE ZONDERVAN CORPORATION
GRAND RAPIDS, MICHIGAN 49506

To the memory of my father-in-law,
Dr. Rolland Roberts Rice

In the years before "modern psychology"
he helped lay the foundation for my wife's
spiritual and moral character. His Christian example
was a deeply meaningful and effective
"Ounce of Prevention."

Acknowledgments

Deep appreciation is extended to my wife Kathy for her consistent support in developing this manuscript and to my secretary Mrs. Joyce Sinclair for her efficient skills in repeatedly deciphering my handwriting and turning it into a readable manuscript.

CONTENTS

CHAPTER ONE

DOES CHRISTIAN TRAINING REALLY WORK?

Flying from one eastern city to another, I busied myself in a local newspaper. The startling headline read CIVIC LEADER MURDERED. After landing I was met by a Christian friend. He said, "Did you read the morning paper?" When I nodded, he replied, "The man was killed by his teenage son. They are both Christians, and the father was active in our church."

As I returned to California, my thoughts turned back to this great tragedy. I began to think of problems of other Christian youth. I remembered the daughter of a missionary family who was living as a prostitute. Then I thought of an outstanding girl, definitely a Christian, who was pregnant and forced to marry. After that I recalled the son of another Christian worker; he was known as the "college drunk" on a Christian college campus. Dozens of others came to mind. All had rather extreme problems and came from Christian homes.

Then I thought of the "milder" problems faced by every parent. Practically all school children cheat at one time or another, and many adolescents go through a period of rebellion. A little of this is normal. But we also know of teenagers from well-respected Christian families who have turned completely against the faith and values of their parents. Drug abuse, teenage pregnancies, and heavy drinking are no longer only the distant life-styles of the non-Christian world. They have planted themselves firmly in the middle of our twentieth century Christian culture.

11

A colleague of mine recently spoke to the freshman class of a well-respected evangelical Christian college. Among other things, this school is known for its strong stand on "Christian separation." In a secret poll he asked how many had smoked marijuana or used some drug illegally during the previous year. To his amazement, more than 60 percent indicated they had! Think of it! Six out of 10 students who had elected to attend a Christian college had at least experimented with drugs during the previous year! Obviously, many of these were one- or two-time trials. But many surely went beyond that point.

For decades we've thought having a "Christian home" would insure the stability of our youth. But rampant problems and rebellion among Christian adolescents shoot this theory full of holes. Apparently there are serious failings, even in our Christian homes. For some reason we have difficulty making our Christian training stick. Children often accept our values for a while but later turn from their Christian training.

Every Christian parent is concerned for his child's spiritual and emotional development. If our Christian faith is real, we want our children to learn certain moral and spiritual values. We want them to acknowledge Christ as Personal Savior, to learn a biblical set of moral guides, and to work out their faith in a meaningful life experience. But while most of us share these goals, we are also well aware that many children fail to live up to their parents' expectations.

THE FAILURE OF FORMAL CHRISTIAN EDUCATION

The same seems true for other forms of Christian guidance. Most of us are committed to the church. We believe Sunday school attendance has a positive influence, and we know people whose lives have been radically turned about by an encounter with Jesus Christ. Many of us have had ministers and Sunday school teachers who made lasting impressions on our lives. Unfortunately, such changes often don't occur. And when they do, their influence often touches only a few areas of our lives. Many who spend months and even years in Christian churches turn out to be little different from the unchurched.

These experiences lead us to ask, "Just how effective are our churches and Sunday schools in changing the attitudes and actions of attenders?" We know tens of thousands of children are being brought to a saving knowledge of Christ as Savior, but what of their lives after this conversion? Is the church really doing an effective job of training children for personal living? Is the typical Christian really that different from the typical non-Christian?

To answer this question, a number of psychologists, sociologists, and educators have carried out numerous research studies. They have compared Christian and non-Christian groups to see what objective differences do exist. Here are the results of a few of these objective studies. Psychiatrist O. S. Walters[1] compared the parents of a group of alcoholics under treatment to the parents of a control group of non-alcoholics. He found that mothers of the alcoholics were *more* active in religious activities than mothers of the non-alcoholics. Smith[2] found that the majority of a group of inmates at a state reformatory had been *regular* church attenders, had studied the Bible in church schools, and had come from church-attending families. Other researchers[3,4] have found that religious people tend to be more prejudiced than non-religious people. Many similar studies suggest Christians are actually inferior to non-Christians in some dimensions of psychological adjustment.

On the positive side, David Moberg[5] found that institutionalized aged people who had been and were still active in religious activities were more likely to be happy than those who had not been active in religious affairs. Another study[6] indicated that children from religious homes were slightly better adjusted than those from less religious homes.

These and other studies are somewhat contradictory. Some research indicates those from religious homes have advantages in adjustment while others suggest religious people are somewhat

1 O. S. Walters, "The Religious Background of Fifty Alcoholics," *Quarterly J. Stud. Alcohol* 18 (1957):405-16.
2 P. M. Smith, "Prisoners' Attitudes Toward Organized Religion," *Religious Education* 51 (1956):462-64.
3 S. B. Blum and J. H. Mann, "The Effect of Religious Membership on Religious Prejudice," *Journal of Social Psychology* 52 (1960):97-101.
4 R. Eiseman and S. W. Cole, "Prejudice and Conservatism in Denominational College Students," *Psychological Reports* 14 (1964):644.
5 David Moberg, "Religious Activities and Personal Adjustment in Old Age," *Journal of Social Psychology* 43 (1956):261-67.
6 Leo Srole et al., *Mental Health in the Metropolis: Midtown Manhattan Study,* vol. 1 (New York: McGraw-Hill Book Co., 1962).

less well adjusted. These few studies serve to illustrate an important point. *In spite of our strong wishes and expectations to the contrary, there is no clear objective, scientific evidence that religious training and beliefs make people significantly different!* Let me clarify this thought a bit. I am not saying that salvation and Christian living are of no consequence. And I am not saying that a vast number of Christians have not had radical life changes. What I am saying is: the objective research of professional psychologists and educators has not shown religious people in general and Christians in particular to be significantly superior to non-Christians in adjustment.

At first glance this may seem startling. And frankly, the present state of research leaves much to be desired. Little research has been done on a well-selected group of evangelical Christians. I imagine that better studies might show more positive results for Christians. On the other hand, it seems clear that whatever differences do exist are not so large as we would hope.

When we think about it further, however, these findings shouldn't really surprise us. How many of us have made clearly observable behavioral and attitudinal changes as a result of our Christian experience? Don't most of us continue to lose our tempers, worry excessively, get depressed, nag our wives, and gossip about our neighbors? In other words, if we are honest, don't we all have to admit our own lives may not be greatly different from our non-Christian neighbors'? Oh, I realize we have an assurance of eternity in heaven. And I know we adhere to certain external indicators of spiritual commitment. And we worship and pray frequently. But what about real, inner personality changes? How many of us are really different because of our Christian faith? Don't most of us fall far short of the Christian ideals we accept as guiding principles for our lives? And don't we know that in a great many cases our churches and Sunday schools have done little more than impart some basic biblical knowledge without really instilling life-changing truths?

In stressing the problems of the home and church, I don't mean to imply that all Christian training is ineffective. And I certainly don't mean to say that Christian homes are worse than others. We are all aware of many wonderful Christian homes and many positive, lasting influences of the church. What I am saying is

14

this: far too many Christian parents are suffering deep heartbreak over the spiritual deadness of their children. As we step further into an age of secularism and humanism, we can expect these problems to increase.

This raises some important questions. It forces us to ask —

"How effective is the church and Sunday school in instilling Christian character?"

"What is the mission of the church?"

"Whose responsibility is it to train children in the nurture and admonition of the Lord?"

I believe the answers to these questions are clear. In answer to the first question, the church is often grossly ineffective in instilling lasting Christian character. As to the second, the major mission of the church is *not* to instill Christian character in our children. Instead, the church's work is equipping the saints and reaching out to the unsaved. And the third: the responsibility for Christian nurture actually belongs to the parents.

In a provocative book entitled *Brethren, Hang Loose,* a pastor comments on the failure of our Christian education programs. In a section called "The Sunday School Illusion" he writes:

> Will a half-decade more be enough to reverse the church's mistaken thinking regarding Christian education? For more than a century, the church and its parents have been deceiving themselves. They have been living and laboring with the empty illusion that the Sunday school can and is doing the job of training their children in the fear and nurture of the Lord.
>
> It's a lie most of us have accepted without question.
>
> It was never a part of God's perfect plan for the church that an artificial agency handle the spiritual education of children. He has a plan. His plan is 4,000 years old. His plan, when put into practice, works. Our poor substitutes for His plan have not worked well even though we have mustered an impressive mountain of statistical and emotional evidence to prove otherwise. The facts are that our children are woefully lacking in both the content and practical applications of God's truth.
>
> God's plan is outlined in Deuteronomy 6:6-9. It lays the burden of teaching and training children where it belongs, in the setting where it can be done most effectively and consistently.
>
> I pray that it will not take five years for the families of our church to come away from dependence upon Sunday school

for the spiritual training of our children. I will be happy to dance on its grave in sheer joy at the knowledge that Christian families are functioning as they were created to for the primary units of spiritual life and growth of family members. I will rejoice to see Sunday school fade away because parents have seen the truth about its inadequacy and have taken the teaching of God's truth into their own hands and are sharing as families in worship, study, prayer and communion.[7]

This view may be a little extreme, but it focuses on a vital point. The Bible places the job of child training squarely on the shoulders of the parents. In this process the church obviously has a supportive role. And in the case of non-Christian homes, the church may play a substitutive role. But in God's plan, parents are intended to do the Christian training. If our children are to develop meaningful Christian values and beliefs, we must accept the challenge of providing them that needed training.

This book is written for the concerned Christian parent. Most of our children will not turn into college drunks, take up employment as prostitutes, or become addicted to dangerous drugs. Instead, the majority of them will mature into average citizens. They will become respected members of their local communities and live "normal" kinds of lives. Surely they will have some problems, but who doesn't? A few problems are to be expected. But as our children move toward maturity, we as Christian parents are still concerned. We want our children to go beyond a normal, humdrum existence. We want them to place Christ at the center of their lives. We want them to be happy and well adjusted. In short, we want them to have that extra "plus factor" that comes from a vital Christian faith.

If we are to instill a deeply meaningful, life-lasting Christian faith, I believe we must take specific steps. We cannot lay our failures at the foot of the church or Sunday school. If we are to accomplish our desires as Christian parents, we must zero in on our own behavior and our own methods of Christian training. Christian training will work if it's really *biblical* training. Proverbs says, "Train up a child in the way he should go: and when he is old, he will not depart from it" (Prov. 22:6). This training involves more than imparting biblical knowledge; it actually involves

[7] Robert C. Girard, *Brethren, Hang Loose* (Grand Rapids: Zondervan Publishing House, 1972), pp. 206-7.

our whole life-style and all our relationships with our children. This book attempts to give some basic parental guidelines for effective spiritual training. It traces some causes for failures in Christian training and offers practical principles for instilling a healthy set of biblical attitudes and actions.

APPLICATION

The story is told of a child psychologist who began his practice with four theories and no children. Some years later he found he had four children and no theories! I'm sure this happens more often than we know. It is one thing to have some abstract knowledge; it is quite another to apply that knowledge to daily life's events.

If reading a book could change our lives, most of us would soon be saints. Unfortunately, we don't function this way. It takes time and experience to learn new patterns of reacting. Only as we gain new understanding, try new techniques, and gradually adapt them to our own environments and personalities do lasting changes come.

The "application" portions of this book are designed to help you apply some general principles of spiritual training to your individual family life. By making concrete applications to your family's needs, you can get beyond a mere intellectual grasp of Christian training to a practical, transforming way of life.

Before going on, let me give a word of caution. Some of these application exercises are easy to complete. They give positive suggestions for spiritual training or suggest a basic evaluation of some attitudes or disciplinary actions. They require no special emotional energy or growth. Other exercises are very different. Since our reactions are the most important determinants of our children's growth, some exercises cut deeply into our own personality attitudes and child-rearing practices. Some people enjoy this.

When they see an area of personal weakness or needed growth, they immediately set out to correct the problem. They seem to delight in new horizons and opportunities for change.

Others of us react another way. As soon as we pause to take stock of areas of needed growth, we begin to experience feelings of anxiety. We think, "It must be hopeless. The more I read the worse I think I am." This attitude is diabolical. It increases personal frustration and short-circuits the desire to grow by making us feel like failures.

Still others go to the opposite extreme. They can't acknowledge any major needs; they say they're satisfied the way they are. In the area of child rearing, they go on "doing what comes naturally." They may have many good attitudes and be adequate parents, but inwardly they're afraid to stop and evaluate their lives. They rationalize by saying, "Things are fine," "I'm too busy," "Child rearing is a woman's job," or "I don't need someone to tell me how to raise my kids!" Underneath these attitudes is fear. These persons don't want to re-evaluate their lives for fear of being found wrong. At an unconscious level they sense the tension that would come with such an honest self-evaluation. Needless to say, this attitude inhibits personal growth.

A healthy attitude toward growth is laid out in the Scriptures. We should always be willing to acknowledge our sins and look at our need for growth. The Bible makes this clear in passages like 1 John 1:5-10 and Ephesians 4:11-16. They teach that we all have sins and we are deceiving ourselves if we think otherwise. But we shouldn't let our sins get us under a pile. The Apostle John writes:

> My little children, I am telling you this so that you will stay away from sin. But if you sin, there is someone to plead for you before the Father. His name is Jesus Christ, the one who is all that is good and who pleases God completely. He is the one who took God's wrath against our sins upon himself, and brought us into fellowship with God; and he is the forgiveness for our sins, and not only ours but all the world's.
>
> (1 John 2:1, 2 *Living Bible*)

In other words, Christ has already paid for our sins and weaknesses, the Holy Spirit is empowering us to grow, and in eternity we will finally become perfectly mature. Meanwhile, we should be sensitive to our needs for growth and willing to take the necessary steps to change. But this change doesn't come overnight.

19

God has set up a universe of principles for healing. Thirty or forty years of habit usually do not suddenly fall away. Instead, God uses His Word, the Holy Spirit, and other people to move us toward a mature life. Because of this it is necessary to gain God's guidance on child training, be sensitive to the Holy Spirit, and interact with other parents.

We often need the help and encouragement of others to overcome long-standing negative feelings and reactions. James 5:16 says:

> Confess your faults one to another, and pray one for another, that ye may be healed. The effectual fervent prayer of a righteous man availeth much.

In Galatians 6:2 Paul writes:

> Share each other's troubles and problems, and so obey our Lord's command. *(Living Bible)*

In other words, God uses people to help us grow. If you run into a barrier in your parent-child relationships, discuss it with a friend. If the problem remains unsolved, seek counseling from a professionally trained person. Psychologists and family counselors are trained to help work out just this type of nitty-gritty problem.

This chapter has discussed the problem of instilling lasting Christian values in our children. We have seen that in spite of our deep concern for the moral and spiritual welfare of our children, many of us fail. This section is designed to help you evaluate some of the reasons Christian training may be ineffective.

EXERCISE I

It is often easier to see the dynamics of the parent-child relationship by beginning with a neutral party. With your husband or wife, discuss one teenager or adult you know who was reared in a Christian home and who has failed to develop a mature Christian commitment. Without a spirit of negative criticism, try to understand his problems.

A. Begin by listing the unhealthy attitudes and actions this person displays.

1. ....

2. . . . .

3. . . . .

4. . . . .

5. . . . .

B. What are some of the parents' strong points in terms of their Christian character and child rearing?

1. . . . .

2. . . . .

3. . . . .

4. . . . .

5. . . . .

C. Often the casual observer doesn't see beyond a Christian family's outward appearance. If a Christian couple are friendly and committed, we assume they are good parents. But this often isn't true. Beneath the outward appearances subtle hostile attitudes, domineering or restrictive actions, excessive involvement in church activities at the expense of children, and other negative behaviors may slowly program Christian children for rebellion. What parental attitudes or actions (subtle or obvious) do you think may have hindered this person's spiritual and moral growth?

1. . . . .

2. . . . .

3. . . . .

4. . . . .

5. ....

D. Sometimes one child "turns out well," and another child from the same family has serious emotional or spiritual problems. If that is true in the family you are discussing, what do you think accounts for it?

1. ....

2. ....

3. ....

4. ....

5. ....

EXERCISE II

Now discuss a family whose children have all "turned out well."
A. Begin by listing some of the spiritual and personal attributes of the children.

1. ....

2. ....

3. ....

4. ....

5. ....

B. What about the parents do you think accounts for the positive growth of their offspring — both in their overall personalities and their specific spiritual training?

1. ....

2. ....

3. ....

4. ....

5. ....

EXERCISE III

Another way of seeing the effect of spiritual training is to recall our own experiences. Discuss with your mate and then complete the following questions.

A. What specific parental actions moved you toward a positive spiritual commitment? Include here important parental attitudes as well as specific spiritual training or experiences.

1. ....

2. ....

3. ....

4. ....

5. ....

B. What family experiences tempted you to rebel or gave your Christian experience a negative or a boring tone? Include faulty parental attitudes and poor family relationships as well as specific negative religious experiences.

1. ....

2. ....

3. ....

4. ....

5. ....

C. What specific extra-family experiences encouraged your spiritual and moral growth? (Include church activities, friends, etc.)

1. ....

2. ....

3. ....

4. ....

5. ....

D. What extra-family experiences discouraged your spiritual and moral growth? (Include bad experiences with churches or Christians, the influence of unsaved friends, etc.)

1. ....

2. ....

3. ....

4. ....

5. ....

CHAPTER TWO

PARENT PRIORITIES

An airline pilot on a transcontinental flight spoke over the loud-speaker saying, "Ladies and gentlemen, I have some mixed news for you tonight. Some of the news is good and some is bad. First, the bad news — our instruments are out and we've lost our way. We're not sure where we're going.... Now for the good news — I'm happy to report we're making excellent time!"

Many of us are like this pilot. As parents we're not sure of our destination but we're getting there in a hurry! We are thrilled when a new baby arrives. We cuddle him and listen to his baby coos. Soon he leaves this stage; almost overnight he begins to grow. In no time at all he's crawling. Soon he's walking and mumbling his first few words. Before long he's five and off to school. We're thrilled with this new venture — but we realize we've lost a baby. Our son is growing up. Soon he enters junior high. Then comes his first date. In a few more years he's off to college and, before we know it, he is gone. We've left our imprint, and now he's on his own.

A heartbroken parent told me recently, "I kept putting off my children. I thought we had years to shape their lives, but now they're nearly grown. We've let our most influential opportunities slip through our fingers."

This testimony is much too common. Its truth is confirmed by psychologists who find the early years of life crucial to all later personal adjustments. Some say our basic personalities are formed in the first five years of life. While this is somewhat debatable, there is no doubt that the preteen years lay the basic groundwork for adult adjustment.

The foundation for moral and spiritual training is our own set of priorities. There come times for each of us when we need to reflect carefully on our style of living and ask ourselves some fundamental questions. For us as Christian parents, one of these questions should surely be, "What are the most important things in life to me?" Obviously, our children will rank high in our answers to this question. But we need to go beyond this verbal assent and demonstrate the importance of our children. We should follow this first question with one like, "Do my daily actions and activities clearly show the high value I place on my children?"

No parent wakes up in the morning thinking, "What can I do to neglect my child today?" Or, "How can I arrange my schedule to ignore my child's spiritual needs and put my other duties first?"

But while none of us would think this way, we often achieve these same results. That is really easy to understand. When we don't wash the dishes, they greet us in the morning. When we let the housework go, it stares us in the face. And when we fail to mow the lawn, we see the results in a week or two. Since these inanimate tasks make their neglect so immediately painful, we give them top priority. But child behavior is different. When we put children off, we may not see results for many years. Only during adolescence or adulthood do some of the ill effects arise. Because of this we are unknowingly duped into setting our precious children aside in favor of a dish, a rug, a weed, or another committee meeting!

Reversed priorities are one of Satan's greatest weapons. Every parent wants to do right by his children. But if we can be subtly led into a life-style that ties up much of our time in secondary activities, Satan has won his war. To correct this trend we need to do some specific planning for our children. Rather than thinking and praying generally for their growth and health, we need to be specific. It's one thing to hope or pray for a "fine Christian boy." It's quite another matter to instill an attitude of Love for God, concern for others, and the ingredients of mature emotional adjustment.

Before discussing specific concepts and techniques of spiritual training, we should give careful thought to our parental goals. This chapter discusses ten basic goals that can move us a long way toward effective spiritual and moral training. While they don't encompass all parental aspirations, they do cover a great deal of ground and may serve as a framework for the rest of our discussions.

TO EXPERIENCE GOD'S LOVE PERSONALLY

Human life has two sides. On the one hand we have thoughts, ideas, and knowledge — in short, intelligence. On the other we have feelings and lively affects — in short, emotions. Balanced living requires both thoughts and feelings. It's one thing to know *about* another person . . . to know his height, his weight, his looks and thoughts. It's another to be in love.

The same is true with God. It's one thing to *know* God intellectually. Many people recite His attributes: He is loving, He is kind, He is just. He is omnipotent and He is omniscient. But it's another thing to *feel* His love.

A personal, experiential awareness of God's love is the foundation of all other goals of spiritual training. If our children can experience God's love through us, they will be able to respond to Him spontaneously. The Bible says the personal experience of being loved by people has a direct carry-over to our experience of God's love. 1 John 4:11, 12 illustrates this principle.

> Dear friends, since God loved us as much as that, we surely ought to love each other too. For though we have never yet seen God, when we love each other God lives in us and His love within us grows ever stronger. *(Living Bible)*

Just recently we had two experiences that illustrate the joys and difficulties of showing children God's love for them. One evening Dickie and Debbie kept interrupting as I was working on this manuscript. I suggested alternate activities, to no avail. Frustrated by my plans being upset, I finally told them sharply to leave the room. They knew I was upset and were probably feeling, "Daddy doesn't love us. He's more interested in his book." And frankly, at that time, I was. But as I recognized their need for attention I laid aside my studies and took some time to work on Dickie's puzzle. Kathy spent some time with Debbie. Soon they were satisfied and went happily off to bed. Then we returned to work, thinking of the many ways we subtly tell our children, "I'm really not interested in you now."

Several days later Dickie and I were spending a lot of time together. We built some buildings out of Legos, worked in the yard, went downtown for a taco and in many ways expressed our mutual affection. As we walked toward the car, Dickie looked up at me with a big smile, and to the tune of the Christian chorus "Every Day With Jesus" started singing, "Every day with Daddy is sweeter than the day before." He knew the real words were "Every day with Jesus" but he tied the two images together. His happy feeling toward me was intimately carried over to his view of God.

This doesn't mean we drop everything each time our children enter the room. We all need time alone and have duties requiring immediate attention. But we should be careful of the quick tendency to say, "I'm busy right now," when children look for

28

our affection. If we find we're *often* too busy, we may need to drastically revise our schedules. Jesus made time for little children in the middle of His busy days. When the disciples rebuked some people for bringing children to see Him, Jesus was displeased and said, "Let the children come to me, for the Kingdom of God belongs to such as they" (Mark 10:14 *Living Bible*).

TO SEE GOD'S WORKING IN THE WORLD AND IN THEIR PERSONAL LIVES

An experiential knowledge of God's love needs to be followed by an understanding of God's daily leading and working in the world. This includes a knowledge of God's involvement in history and in current international affairs.

During the 1972 Olympics we watched our television sets intently as the Arab guerrillas took Israeli athletes hostage. For hours we wondered what would happen. Finally the report came to the newscasters — all hostages had been killed. The effect on the news reporters was upsetting in itself. They were completely at a loss; for moments no one spoke. Finally they uttered a few feeble comments about the lack of appropriate words on such occasions. As a Christian I was again reminded of the utter sense of frustration the non-Christian feels in the face of such a tragedy. He has no understanding of the biblical backdrop for such seemingly senseless killings.

Although our family participated deeply in the sorrow, we also knew this sort of action would continue. We knew we were living in a sinful world and that no amount of "international good will" would solve the problem of sinful human nature.

Just a few nights before this tragedy Kathy was reading Dickie the story of Ishmael and Isaac. She read how Ishmael was a son of Abraham by his handmaid Hagar and how Isaac was Abraham's son by his wife Sarah. She read[1] how Ishmael and his mother were sent into the wilderness because of the conflict between the two children. And she told how Ishmael became a famous archer and eventually became the father of the Arab nations. During the televised Olympic drama we had an opportunity to point out how the fights between Isaac and Ishmael centuries ago were

---

[1] Kathy was reading from *Taylor's Bible Story Book*, written by Ken Taylor and published by Tyndale House Publishers, Wheaton, Illinois. The biblical record of these interesting events is covered in Genesis 16:1–25:17.

just the beginning of the conflicts we were seeing in 1972. We also pointed out that just this kind of problem was prophesied long ago. We went on to tell our children how the Arab-Israeli conflict was a part of God's program of restoring Israel to its native soil and preparing for Christ's second coming.

The Bible says God has an active superintending influence in all of world affairs![2] By sharing insights about His working we do much to give our children a biblical perspective and a Christian view of life.

Bible stories have much the same effect. The Old Testament is filled with exciting human interest stories that clearly spell out God's plan for the human race, the results of sin, the conflict between good and evil, and the eventual victory of the good. The deeply personal experiences of men like David, Abraham, and Joseph bring a deep sense of identification and involvement from our children and help instill important Christian concepts.

TO COME TO A PERSONAL COMMITMENT TO JESUS CHRIST

A general influence of Christian love and teaching is essential for our children. But by itself it's not enough. Children need to be led to a personal acceptance of Christ as Savior. Yet in doing this we must avoid two extremes. Some of us want to push children into a commitment to Christ in the first few years of life; we would like to hear them say, "I was saved at three!" But during this period it's doubtful that a child understands the abstract concepts of sin, heaven, hell, and death. He may be making genuine steps toward God, but until he reaches six or older he isn't ready to comprehend the basic elements of salvation. This doesn't mean we should minimize spontaneous reactions to God before that time. An understanding of right and wrong, of justice, and of His fatherly love should begin early in life. What I am saying is this: we should not try to bring a child to a specific commitment to Christ until he really understands the issues.

At the opposite end of the spectrum are parents who hesitate to ask their child about a salvation experience. They don't want to "cram something down his throat," and they want it to be "his

---

[2] Romans 13:1, "Let every soul be subject unto the higher powers. For there is no power but of God: the powers that be are ordained of God."
Daniel 4:17b, "...the most High ruleth in the kingdom of men, and giveth it to whomsoever he will, and setteth up over it the basest of men."

decision." This thinking is good, but it shouldn't keep us from a frank talk with our children about the plan of salvation and their response to it. By the time a child is eight or ten we certainly should have had one or more clear discussions on his response to God's salvation.

A friend of ours recently related the following incident:

> It was Thursday evening and I was scheduled to go out for supper with my husband. Since we didn't do this often I was really looking forward to it. About the time he should have been getting home I got a call from my husband. He had to go to some "important" company meeting. I was so disappointed and angry I threw the whole bunch of socks I was rolling into the drawer. I just felt like sulking for a while.
>
> Then I asked myself what perspective the Lord would want me to have. I knew it would be one of giving thanks and having a positive attitude. So intellectually at least I began to thank the Lord for these circumstances.
>
> Later that evening I was sitting on the couch when my eight-year-old daughter came and sat beside me. We talked about her day and had a good visit. Pretty soon she said, 'Mommy, how can I be good instead of bad and stay that way?' I explained to her how she could invite Jesus to come and take over her life and how He would give her the power to want to be good. We knelt down together while she made this eternal decision.
>
> Later I thought how valuable this unplanned time had been. I vowed to do my best to always be available to my children.

This experience illustrates several important points. If we are going to lead our children to Christ, we must have open lines of communication. We must be willing to take time with them. And we must be prepared to show them God's plan for their lives.

TO DEVELOP A SENSE OF MISSION

Most of us have a desire for Christian service. We see a needy world and want to do our part in reaching it for Christ.[3] We also want our children to value other people, to witness, and to find their role in the work of the church. But how does this come about? What can we do to help our children want to witness? Very basically, this will come from our example and involvement. Some mothers sponsor Child Evangelism classes in their homes.

---

[3] Matthew 28:19, 20, "Go ye therefore, and teach all nations, baptizing them in the name of the Father, and of the Son, and of the Holy Ghost: teaching them to observe all things whatsoever I have commanded you: and, lo, I am with you alway, even unto the end of the world. Amen."

This is an excellent way of reaching neighborhood children; it also involves our own children in a spiritual ministry.[4] We may take our children with us when witnessing to an unsaved family. We may pray for unsaved neighbors. And we may witness and take a neighbor's children with us to Sunday school. Inviting missionaries and other Christian workers into our homes is another good way to promote a positive interest in evangelism and Christian service. As we spontaneously engage in these and other Christian outreaches, our children will pick up our vision for serving Christ.

TO BE HAPPY

All parents want happy children. We want them to have a positive outlook on life and avoid any serious maladjustments. But we often fail to consider this a spiritual concern. We segment our thinking into the "psychological" and the "spiritual." Sometimes we are doing "spiritual training"; other times we are working on "emotions." This is a false dichotomy. Personal happiness and emotional health are essential to an effective spiritual commitment. One of the fruits of the Spirit is joy.[5] Christ said He came to give us life abundantly[6] and Psalm 37:4 says

> Delight thyself also in the Lord; and he shall give thee the desires of thine heart.

In other words, God sees our children's personal happiness as a vital spiritual concern.

Our whole way of living sets the pattern for our children's self-acceptance. While this side of personal mental health is beyond the scope of our present concern, let me raise a few questions that may help us check on our reactions and their influence on our children; they may serve as a quick emotional thermometer. Since this book focuses little on emotional adjustment, you may want to read some other writings on that topic.[7]

---

[4] You may obtain information on Child Evangelism classes by writing Child Evangelism Fellowship, Inc., P.O. Box 1156, Grand Rapids, MI 49501.

[5] Galatians 5:22, "But the fruit of the Spirit is love, joy, peace, longsuffering, gentleness, goodness, faith."

[6] John 10:10b, "I am come that they might have life, and that they might have it more abundantly."

[7] Here are two books which deal with broader issues of child adjustment:

(1) Haim G. Ginott, *Between Parent and Child* (New York: Avon Books, 1965).

(2) Rudolf Dreikurs and Loren Grey, *Logical Consequences: A New Approach to Discipline* (New York: Hawthorn Books, Inc., 1968).

1. Is our family life often in a state of tension?
2. Do I often become angry and upset and emphasize my children's faults?
3. Does my child often feel deprived of wanted pleasures because we are a "Christian family"?
4. Does our family spend many enjoyable recreation times together?
5. Does my child *feel* I love him *all* the time? It's one thing to love our children. It's another thing to be sure they understand and accept our love.

Some time ago I counseled a young married man. He was raised in a "good Christian home," and his father was a pastor. Although the parents had a satisfactory marriage and thought they had a decent family life, this boy became seriously rebellious. He drank heavily, married a non-Christian, and turned against his Christian faith. In telling me how he resented the great amounts of time his father spent at the church, this young man told how during a drinking party he lifted a beer to his lips and proclaimed, "Here's one for the deacon's board!"

This man had received a lot of Christian training. His parents were sincere and loved their children. But he felt pushed aside for the ministry of the church. This feeling and other subtle emotional problems in the home drove him from his parents as well as God. This experience is all too common. Unless we are meeting our children's emotional needs, we will have difficulty making our Christian training work.

TO INTERNALIZE BIBLICAL STANDARDS OF MORALITY

A code of moral values is crucial to a mature spiritual life. But effective Christian training involves much more than an intellectual assent to a biblical creed. To be effective, Christian standards must become a part of our children's inner lives. The children must come to see biblical standards as personally meaningful and relevant rather than as arbitrary regulations imposed by the church.

Biblical truth is truth, but it may be presented in many ways. We may naively say, "We do this because the Bible says so." Or we may take time to discuss our children's feelings and gently point out the reasons for biblical standards. The first approach instills a negative view of Christian living; the latter builds healthy Christian attitudes. The biblical motive for obedience is love, not forced conformity. John 14:15 says, "If ye love me, keep my commandments." Carefully presented biblical principles take on much deeper life-meaning than rigidly imposed external expectations. Chapters four through seven deal specifically with ways of teaching biblical standards and promoting our children's moral growth.

TO DEVELOP GOOD RELATIONSHIPS WITH OTHERS

Another ingredient of maturity is good interpersonal relations. For myself, I don't care whether my children are outgoing and gregarious or rather quiet and thoughtful. These traits are influenced by many factors including innate dispositions. But I do want them to feel secure in personal relationships and to enjoy their times with other people.

Some parents pay little attention to their children's friendships. They fail to realize the strong influence of childhood peer relationships. Good friendships lay a foundation for healthy adult interpersonal relations. Dealings with the wrong playmates may set patterns for spiteful, jealous relationships and may also turn our children's attention to unnecessary sexual experimentation and "gutter language." Because of this, the Bible places a strong emphasis on the influence of friends. Wise parents follow this advice and help their children develop positive childhood friendships. Listen to a few key comments from the Scriptures (all from the Living Bible):

> Don't envy godless men; don't even enjoy their company. (Prov. 24:1)
> Be with wise men and become wise. Be with evil men and become evil. (Prov. 13:20)
> A mirror reflects a man's face, but what he is really like is shown by the kind of friends he chooses. (Prov. 27:19)
> Wounds from a friend are better than kisses from an enemy! (Prov. 27:6)
> A friendly discussion is as stimulating as the sparks that fly when iron strikes iron. (Prov. 27:17)
> This will make possible the next step, which is for you to enjoy other people and to like them, and finally you will grow to love them deeply. The more you go on in this way, the more you will grow strong spiritually and become fruitful and useful to our Lord Jesus Christ. (2 Pet. 1:7, 8)

Some parents go overboard in trying to implement these concepts. From early life they teach their children, "We're Christians so we're different. We must be separate," or "We should be careful about the friends we choose." All this is true. But improperly understood it may cause what I call "evangelical paranoia." Our children become frightened of the non-Christian world. They think, "Non-Christians make fun of us and want no part of us." Or, "If we witness, we'll be rejected and persecuted." In short, they feel odd, isolated, persecuted, and rejected because of their faith in Christ.

This is a terribly unhealthy view of Christianity. It distorts the true meaning of Christian separation and may lead to neurotic personal adjustment. We must help our children develop confidence and deep, intimate friendships while being sensitive to unnecessary negative peer influences. We will accomplish this only as we have meaningful, honest, open, and loving relationships both with our neighbors and with our Christian friends.

Sometimes we must go out of our way to do this. We may have to drive across town to take our children to a Christian playmate's home. We may need to change churches so that our teenagers can be with a group of sharp Christian young people. Or we may need to have some good talks with our children about their activities and their choice of friends.

TO AVOID AS MANY CONSEQUENCES OF SIN AS POSSIBLE WITHOUT BEING OVERLY SHELTERED

All of us inwardly hurt when we see our children suffer from their sins. We try to guide them and set limits to protect them. But we also realize they can't mature unless we let them make their own decisions.

We need to learn to control our children when that is required. to give them guidance at other times, and to allow them to make their own mistakes when that is necessary. Only as we strike a proper balance between control, guidance, and freedom will our children develop a sense of identity and personal responsibility. Our responsibility is to guide our children without robbing them of the chance to make their own decisions and to accept responsibility for their own actions.

TO DEVELOP AN APPRECIATION FOR LIFE AND NATURE

God has created a fascinating and beautiful world, and it's

important for children to develop their aesthetic senses. Music, art, and nature all provide needed uplifting and enjoyment. As we help our children appreciate His creation, we are helping with both their spiritual and emotional growth. Without forcing our own specific interests onto our children, we should try to help them develop their God-given gifts and aesthetic interests.[8]

TO BE SUCCESSFUL AND DEVELOP LEADERSHIP ABILITY

This one is a sticky wicket. Everyone wants successful children. But I for one am prone to overemphasize achievement. While my children may happen to develop superior athletic ability or academic skills, I'm a little too ego-involved in their performance. I have to be careful not to push them to meet my standards or to pressure them to grow at my desired speed.

Each of us needs to be sensitive to our children's abilities so we may encourage and guide their development without forcing or coercing them to meet our own standards. As we look around the church we see God using all sorts of people and all kinds of gifts. Some people are aggressive leaders; others are helpful followers. Some are talented musically, while others can hardly sing a note. Some have the gift of teaching, others the gift of hospitality.[9] One of the most rewarding experiences a Christian parent can have is the joy of seeing the gradual unfolding of his child's divinely given talents and the channeling of these talents into the service of Christ and His church.

SUMMARY

This concludes our survey of suggested goals for spiritual training. These goals are obviously broad. It's impossible to isolate

[8] Edith Schaeffer has written an excellent book along this line. The book, *Hidden Art,* is published by Tyndale House (Wheaton, 1972). Every mother should read this stimulating book.
[9] Ephesians 4:7, 11-13, "However, Christ has given each of us special abilities — whatever he wants us to have out of his rich storehouse of gifts.... Some of us have been given special ability as apostles; to others he has given the gift of being able to preach well; some have special ability in winning people to Christ, helping them to trust him as their Savior; still others have a gift for caring for God's people as a shepherd does his sheep, leading and teaching them in the ways of God. Why is it that he gives us these special abilities to do certain things best? It is that God's people will be equipped to do better work for him, building up the church, the body of Christ, to a position of strength and maturity; until finally we all believe alike about our salvation and about our Savior, God's Son, and all become full-grown in the Lord — yes, to the point of being filled full with Christ" (*Living Bible*).

spiritual training from other areas of life. If our children are to develop into mature Christian people, they will need our vital involvement in every area of life. The important point is this: when we're going on a journey, we get a map. We have a goal in mind, and we make periodic checks on our progress. Likewise, Christian training is a journey. We pass through various stages and need directions at various times. To be sure we arrive at our chosen destination we need to map out our goals in family living. Then we must make periodic checks to be sure we're making needed progress.

APPLICATION

No parent wakes up in the morning thinking, "What things can I find to do that will allow me to spend less time with my children?" or "What opportunities for spiritual training can I sidestep today?" But unthinkingly each of us does these very things. If we are going to share life-changing spiritual truths effectively with our children, we must make this top priority.

EXERCISE I

Take an evening to discuss some of the major goals you have for your children. Realizing that you have only a few years to influence their lives and set their courses for eternity, list your goals below. Be sure your goals are specific enough to work toward, yet general enough to allow your children great flexibility and spontaneity to develop their unique capacities. After you have finished reading the entire book, come back to this chapter and write the specific steps you want to take to meet your goals.

Goal 1. . . . .

Ways of Meeting It

    1. . . . .

    2. . . . .

    3. . . . .

Goal 2. ....

Ways of Meeting It

    1. ....

    2. ....

    3. ....

Goal 3. ....

Ways of Meeting It

    1. ....

    2. ....

    3. ....

Goal 4. ....

Ways of Meeting It

    1. ....

    2. ....

    3. ....

Goal 5. ....

Ways of Meeting It

    1. ....

    2. ....

    3. ....

Goal 6. ....

Ways of Meeting It

    1. ....

    2. ....

    3. ....

Goal 7. ....

Ways of Meeting It

    1. ....

    2. ....

    3. ....

Goal 8. ....

Ways of Meeting It

    1. ....

    2. ....

    3. ....

EXERCISE II

To place things in perspective, let's divide our day into activity categories to see how much time we spend on certain tasks. This exercise will help us evaluate our parental priorities.

A. For three days make a chart of the approximate amount of time you spend in each of the following activities. If you can't fit all of your day's activities in, add an additional category or two. Fill out the charts (pages 42, 43) for a Saturday, a Sunday, and one weekday. During the week most of us rationalize our schedules by saying, "I'm too busy. On Saturday I'll have more

40

time with the family." Or, "On Sunday we'll have more time for spiritual things." By charting our "free time" of Saturday and Sunday we will gain a balanced picture of our activities. Round off your time to the nearest five minutes.

B. For most of us, work and sleep occupy the majority of our time. And both of these are obviously essential. But what about our other activities? Total your time in spiritual interactions with your children. How does this compare with the amount of time you spend going to meetings, watching television, and

reading the newspaper? . . . .

. . . .

If your deepest priorities don't seem to match the amount of time you spend in other activities, you may need to make some specific changes (like cutting back on television time or unnecessary meetings). Can you find ways of altering your schedule to provide at least three or four uninterrupted hours weekly with your children? This time may be work, play, or devotions. The important thing is the individual attention. In what specific activities are you going to spend less time?

1. . . . .

2. . . . .

3. . . . .

4. . . . .

What do you intend to do with your newly found "extra" hours?

1. . . . .

2. . . . .

3. . . . .

4. . . . .

WIFE'S TIME CHART

ACTIVITY	AMOUNT OF TIME		
	Weekday	Saturday	Sunday
Work (not housework — only for employees)			
Eating (at home or out)			
Preparing meals			
Washing dishes			
All other household duties			
Television			
Yard work and related tasks			
Shopping			
Entertainment (movies, ballgames, church socials, home entertainment, etc.)			
Personal devotions (prayer and Bible study)			
Family devotions			
Correspondence			
Church attendance			
Bathing and getting dressed			
Getting children dressed and off to school or other functions			
Clubs, meetings, teas, etc.			
Driving to and from work or school			
Sleeping			
Reading, resting, etc.			
Uninterrupted playtime with children			
Uninterrupted mutual discussions with children			
Spontaneous discussion of spiritual concepts with children			
Direct witnessing			
Other			
Wasted time, etc.			
TOTAL	24	24	24

HUSBAND'S TIME CHART

ACTIVITY	AMOUNT OF TIME		
	Weekday	Saturday	Sunday
Work (not housework — only for employees)			
Eating (at home or out)			
Preparing meals			
Washing dishes			
All other household duties			
Television			
Yard work and related tasks			
Shopping			
Entertainment (movies, ballgames, church socials, home entertainment, etc.)			
Personal devotions (prayer and Bible study)			
Family devotions			
Correspondence			
Church attendance			
Bathing and getting dressed			
Getting children dressed and off to school or other functions			
Clubs, meetings, teas, etc.			
Driving to and from work or school			
Sleeping			
Reading, resting, etc.			
Uninterrupted playtime with children			
Uninterrupted mutual discussions with children			
Spontaneous discussion of spiritual concepts with children			
Direct witnessing			
Other			
Wasted time, etc.			
TOTAL	24	24	24

CHAPTER THREE

THREE KEYS TO CHRISTIAN TRAINING

All of us are concerned for our children's spiritual future. But we show our concern in different ways. Some of us regularly attend church with our families, say grace before meals, and have a daily time of family devotions. Other parents limit their spiritual activities more to mealtime prayers and church attendance. Still others merely drop their children off at church; they let the professionals do the spiritual work. "After all," they think, "we don't know much about the Bible, and the pastor's paid to be the expert."

Each of these activities has its place. In fact, they may have deep influences on the lives of children. But to be effective, spiritual training must not be limited to these more or less planned, routine times of study and worship. If it is to make a lasting impression, our moral and spiritual training must involve our total life experience. Christian training that is limited to set times of formal worship and instruction is doomed to failure. Consider this Old Testament discussion of family spiritual training:

> And you shall love the Lord your God with all your [mind and] heart, and with your entire being, and with all your might. And these words, which I am commanding you this day, shall be [first] in your own mind and heart; [then] You shall whet and sharpen them, so as to make them penetrate, and teach and impress them diligently upon the [minds and] hearts of your children, and shall talk of them when you sit in your house, and when you walk by the way, and when you lie down and when you rise up. And you shall bind them as a sign upon your hand, and they shall be as frontlets [forehead bands]

45

between your eyes. And you shall write them upon the door-
posts of your house and on your gates.

(Deut. 6:5-9 Amplified Bible)

Notice the two emphases of this passage. First, the older genera-
tion was to be vitally influenced by God in every area of their
lives. They were to love God with their whole beings. Unfortunately, most of us limit God's influence to a few well-defined
areas. We acknowledge Him at meals, at church, in prayer, and
during panic situations. But we fail to see God's hand in our daily
affairs. Even as Christians, most of us conduct our daily duties
much like our non-Christian neighbors. We fail to put our total
life-style into a biblical perspective.

Only after the Israelites personally responded to God's leading
were they to teach their children spiritual truth. That is the
second emphasis. When they did teach, it wasn't a brief mealtime
blessing or a good-night prayer. It was to be a way of life. They
were to teach their children when they sat in the house. They
were to instruct them as they walked outside. And they were to
share spiritual thoughts both in the evenings and in the mornings.

SUNDAY SERVICES

SUNDAY SCHOOL   9:30
MORNING WORSHIP   11:00
EVENING SERVICE   6:00

In other words, effective spiritual training was to be a daily way of life.

These guidelines for spiritual training were written around 1400 B.C., some thirty-four hundred years ago. Yet few thinking people would question the success of this kind of training in the Jewish race. More than any nation in the world, Israel has maintained its cultural and religious heritage. Under extreme pressures and worldwide separation, the Jewish race retains its unity. Much of this is due to the close family ties and the early religious training of the children. We can profit much from the experience of God's chosen nation.

The three keys to Christian training discussed in this chapter have their roots in the approach to spiritual training reflected in God's instruction to the Hebrews in Deuteronomy.

YOUR CHILD'S IMAGE OF GOD

A friend of mine told of an incident he witnessed in Georgia. A young boy from a rural area was brought to church for the first time. It was a good-sized city church with an older pastor, a stately looking gentleman with white hair. As the country boy entered the church and saw the minister in the pulpit, he turned in awe to a friend and asked, "Is that God?"

This little event illustrates a big truth — children first see God through His earthly representatives.

When God decided to create man He had a problem. How was a physical, material person on earth going to comprehend an immaterial God located in a seemingly distant heaven? To bridge the gap it was necessary to teach man something of the character of God and the nature of spiritual truth. He chose to accomplish this by using earthly concepts to illustrate divine truth. God uses light to represent the True Light.[1] He uses the vine to represent the True Vine.[2] And He uses a father to represent the True Father.[3]

---

1 "Then spake Jesus again unto them, saying, I am the light of the world: he that followeth me shall not walk in darkness, but shall have the light of life" (John 8:12).
2 "I am the true vine, and my Father is the husbandman. Every branch in me that beareth not fruit he taketh away: and every branch that beareth fruit, he purgeth it, that it may bring forth more fruit" (John 15:1, 2).
3 "You must submit to and endure [correction] for discipline. God is dealing with you as with sons; for what son is there whom his father does not [thus] train and correct and discipline? Now if you are exempt from correction and left without discipline in which all [of God's children] share, then you are illegitimate offspring

The newborn child has no image of his own parents, let alone a personal God. But as he grows in a normal family situation he develops deep relationships with his mother and his father. He learns the concept "Father." He knows a father is strong and loving; he knows a father protects him and at times may have to discipline and instruct him. As he grows older we can tell him, "God loves you. He is like a heavenly Father." Immediately the child begins to understand. He transfers his image of his earthly father over to the Heavenly Father. This is the beginning of a child's knowledge of God. The carry-over from earthly to Heavenly Father is clearly shown in Matthew 7:11 where Christ says, "If ye then, being evil, know how to give good gifts unto your children, how much more shall your Father which is in heaven give good things to them that ask him?" This passage tells us a child can expect to see the virtues of his parents magnified in his Heavenly Father. Where few of these virtues exist, it is hard to build up a positive image of God.

In describing this process J. B. Phillips writes:

> ... the early conception of God is almost invariably founded upon the child's idea of his father. If he is lucky enough to have a good father this is all to the good, provided of course that the conception of God grows with the rest of personality. But if the child is afraid (or, worse still, afraid and feeling guilty because he is afraid) of his own father, the chances are that his Father in Heaven will appear to him a fearful Being.
>
> Again, if he is lucky, he will outgrow this conception, and indeed differentiate between his early 'fearful' idea and his later mature conception. But many are not able to outgrow the sense of guilt and fear, and in adult years are still obsessed with it, although it has actually nothing to do with their real relationship with the living God. It is nothing more than a parental hangover.[4]

What if parents physically abandon a young child? What if he is sent to an orphanage or bounced from one foster home to another? Because of this he knows no father. He knows men, but he's never had a lasting, loving relationship with an intimate, caring parent. Then he reads the Bible and hears, "You can trust

and not true sons [at all]. Moreover, we have had earthly fathers who disciplined us and we yielded [to them] and respected [them for training us]. Shall we not much more cheerfully submit to the Father of spirits and so [truly] live?" (Heb. 12:7-10 *Amplified Bible*).

[4] J. B. Phillips, *Your God Is Too Small* (New York: The Macmillan Company, 1969), pp. 14-15.

48

your Heavenly Father. He won't let you down!" He finds that difficult to accept. For years he has been mistreated. It isn't easy to throw off all those images and gain a picture of a loving Father.

When we consider that at least one in four marriages ends in divorce, think of the effect. We may assume that on this basis alone nearly one quarter of the children in the United States are deprived of a lasting relationship with their earthly fathers. Most of these children remain under their mothers' custody, and a large proportion of these mothers soon remarry. Yet this doesn't really solve the problem. The trauma of losing a father is not easily overcome by your mother marrying a stranger!

But the problem of developing a healthy relationship with parents that will transfer on to God is not limited to instances of divorce, death, and separation. It actually carries into every home. No parent is perfect. Some of us are overtly hostile and rejecting. Others are very controlled and polite, but fail to get involved with our children; this is especially true for busy men. After a good day's work we come home desiring a little peace and quiet. It is much easier to say to a child, "Dad's busy right now," than it is to get up from the easy chair and spend some time with him.

Many parents are good providers and faithful to their children, but they lack a warm, spontaneous, happy parent-child relationship. I once counseled a fifty-year-old woman who was a fine Christian and active in her church. But she had periods of depression and sometimes found it hard to accept God's love for her. One day she described her earthly father: "He was a fine man. He was honest, fair, and well respected. But I never felt close to him at all." A few weeks later she discussed her feelings toward God. She said, "He is just and kind and loving, but He seems so far away." She used almost the same words to describe her feelings toward her father and toward God!

Other parents have different characteristics. A mother, for example, may be very nervous and easily brought to tears; what may be very normal childish reactions frustrate her continually. This instills in the child a sense of blame for his mother's emotional upset. Or it leads to resentment on his part. He comes to see God as an overly protective, worrisome parent.

These are just a few of the patterns that may place barriers between a growing child and God. These family interactions not

49

Matt. 7:11 - If ye (earthly parents) know how to give good gifts unto your children, how much more shall your Father which is in heaven give good gifts to them that seek Him?

only cause immediate frustrations but also lay down conscious and unconscious impressions toward all authority figures. *Any negative attitude toward a parent may later cause problems in relationships with God.* In a helpful book on spiritual training in the home, Anna Mow puts it this way:

> Real religion is a matter of our life relationships much more than it is a matter of words. We start too late if we begin our teaching about God with *words.* Too many Christians have thought of God in verbal terms only. They are seemingly satisfied with the things that can be said *about* Him. Words are important and have their rightful place but another foundation must come first. *This foundation is built in the relationship of the home.* If the church must bear the brunt of the verbal teaching without this foundation experience in the home it is as if the foundation were built on top of the walls instead of under them.[5]

In two other books[6] I have detailed this carry-over from parents to God in greater depth. Chapters three and four of *A Guide to Child Rearing* contain a set of questions and discussion guides to help parents clarify their own images of God as well as those of their children. A study of that material may be an effective means of gaining deeper insights into your relationship with your children and ways of building a positive foundation for your child's relationship with God.

A SPIRITUAL SEED FROM A GARDEN WEED

A few years ago my son and I were working in the garden. "Did God make weeds, Daddy?" Dickie asked with a puzzled look. I started to give him a quick answer and go on with my work. Then I realized this was an opportunity to teach my son a spiritual lesson. I laid down my weeding fork and said, "Dickie, you know about Adam and Eve. They were the first people that ever lived on earth. God put them in a beautiful garden without *any* weeds. Then one day the devil came along looking like a snake. He told Adam and Eve to disobey God; he said they should eat some fruit God told them not to eat. And you know what happened? They ate it. Then the world started having problems. After Adam and Eve disobeyed God, weeds started growing and

---

[5] Anna B. Mow, *Your Child* (Grand Rapids: Zondervan Publishing House, 1963), p. 23.
[6] Bruce Narramore, *Help! I'm A Parent* and *A Guide to Child Rearing* (Grand Rapids: Zondervan Publishing House, 1972).

they had to go to work and leave their pretty garden. Isn't that a shame? If they'd listened to God we wouldn't have to be out here pulling weeds!" With a pleased look on his face Dickie thoughtfully replied, "Yes, that's too bad."

I relate this little incident to illustrate a vital learning principle. *Lessons arising out of real life experiences are usually much more effective than formal instruction given in an isolated setting.*

Unfortunately, many of us forget the many ways God works. A person told me recently, "God isn't really interested in me and my daily life. He has the whole universe to run." In expressing her feelings this woman was communicating an attitude held by many Christians. Intellectually we "know" God loves us, but it's often hard to "feel" His presence. This attitude comes largely from experiences with our own parents, who sometimes implied, "Don't bother me with little things. We have important things to do!" As we grow up we carry this attitude on to God and think He lacks interest in the little things of life.

The feeling that God isn't vitally interested in our daily affairs is compounded by a tendency to take life for granted. We see the sun rise in the morning and think, "So what? It does that every day." And, of course, it does. But behind this daily routine is the creative power of God. He designed our universe and ordained the complex forces of energy that keep our earth in orbit and the stars in their proper paths. We go through a rainy period and don't stop to remind our children this is God's way of irrigating the plant kingdom and perpetuating the whole life cycle.

Seeing God in nature is just one part of seeing God in every area of life. The important military and political affairs in Israel and the Mideast give excellent opportunities to teach our children spiritual truths. The whole idea of the call of Abraham, the line of the Messiah, the persecution and captivities of the Jewish people and their present restoration to the Promised Land are living demonstrations of the authority of God's Word through fulfilled prophecies.

President Nixon's visit to China opened up new opportunities to talk with our children about the missionary movement and the spiritual condition of other nations. In a similar way, nature's wonders, daily occurrences, and various hardships and disasters all provide vital opportunities to give children a Christian world view that sees God's superintending influence and the conflict of good and evil in all areas of life.

A few years ago Dickie and I were driving downtown. Out of the blue he asked, "Daddy, if you break your arm can you fix it?"

"That's a good question, son," I said, giving myself some time to think. "You know, God made our bodies in a very special way. Inside we have bones that are hard like sticks or boards."

"You mean like a chicken bone, Daddy?"

"Kinda," I answered. "And sometimes when we fall or have an accident we break one of our bones. But God made our bones so they grow back together. A doctor can put our bone together, and after a while God makes it grow real strong again. Isn't that nice!"

"Yes," said Dickie. "God sure is good."

Once again, we used a very simple question as an opportunity to discover a spiritual truth. In this discussion Dickie was learning an important lesson about the power of God who created our intricate bodies with the amazing powers of self-regeneration.

CREATIVE TEACHING

Most of us fall into ruts quite easily. We go through the same rituals day after day. We know our homes so well we can walk the halls blindfolded. We drive the same highways so often it becomes almost automatic. And we develop certain habit forms of speech like "Hi! How are you?" and get the predictable reply, "Fine. How are you?" It we aren't careful, this same routineness can befall our spiritual lives. We repeat almost identical prayers before each meal or end each day with our own version of "Now I lay me down to sleep." Sometimes this routine become so boring it becomes a meaningless ritual. I remember some students at a Christian college who would jokingly bow their heads and count to ten before each meal. They felt the custom of grace had become so routine it had no meaning left!

One evening I came home unusually tired. I fell into bed exhausted but remembered I hadn't had my evening prayer. Being in a weakened condition I prayed, "Lord, thank you for this food. Amen." Then I realized I had prayed the wrong prayer! My internal computer had thrown out a mealtime message instead of a good-night one. How little meaning that evening ritual held.

But this need not be! Times of prayer and Bible study can be unique and enriching experiences.

One evening Dickie wanted his mother to read the story of Absalom. After reading the story from 2 Samuel they decided to act it out. Dickie was four at the time, and Debbie was two years old. My wife's goal was to see if they could catch some of the feelings of the Bible characters by acting out the story. We also hoped we would discover more about the feelings of our little ones. Kathy was the tree — she stretched her arms like branches and took her place. Debbie was Absalom riding on her plastic horse. When she passed by, the tree reached out and grabbed her golden locks. As she hung there, Dickie gleefully shot her with an imaginary bow and arrow. Absalom-Debbie cooperatively thumped to the floor in death. Then they changed roles for the next scene. Kathy became King David, and Dickie was the messenger. They enacted King David's grief over losing his son. After the play was completed, the children wanted to do it again. This time Dickie was the tree, and Debbie shot the fatal arrow at her mother (Absalom).

Another time they dramatized the parable of the good Samaritan. Debbie was the wounded man; she lay in our darkened hall while Kathy played the Samaritan. Dickie, wearing my suit coat, played the Levite and the priest. He happily passed on by, leaving his sister lying in the dark. Because of some sibling rivalry, Dickie found it nearly impossible to be the good Samaritan. He didn't want to help his sister! When pressed by his mother to take another role, the best he could do was be the donkey that carried his sister to the inn!

Another time, after a hot and difficult day, Kathy decided to make a potentially whining suppertime into something different.

She organized a treasure hunt for dinner. She started by giving Dickie and Debbie a little picture showing where the first part of the meal was located. Much to her artistic gratification, they recognized the drawing and went straight to the bathroom sink, where they found two Cokes and the next picture. That clue pointed to the dishwasher, which held their macaroni. On to the oven for dessert and then under the bed, where they found their pajamas readied for them. The final clue led to the porch, where their Bible storybook was hidden. This treasure hunt meal sent two little tired but happy children off to bed with a sense of satisfaction coming from a happy day. Their last memory of that day was an interesting Bible story.

DON'T FORGET THE OBVIOUS

In this chapter we have sought to broaden our horizons. We have demonstrated the importance of our relationships with our children. We have illustrated ways of relating our faith to every part of life. And we have suggested a few creative ways of teaching spiritual truths.

In zeroing in on these frequently neglected areas, I don't want to overlook the obvious. Children do need daily doses of spiritual food. *Mealtime prayers and nighttime stories are excellent vehicles for instilling spiritual concepts.* Each evening our family goes through this routine. Kathy or I (and sometimes both) go to our children's rooms. We use this time to review the day's events, talk a little while, and then we "sing and pray." After singing our children's favorite songs we have a time of conversational prayer. In this way we are having good communication as well as teaching spiritual truths. Besides its spiritual lessons, this routine also has a very effective tranquilizing action!

Formal Christian training also is important. Every parent needs to choose carefully a church and Sunday school. Parents of teenagers may need to re-evaluate their present church home; although they are happy with a church, it may not be meeting their children's total needs. Nothing does more to turn off a sharp teenager than a boring youth program led by a spiritually committed but socially inadequate person! Before we pack our bags, our first thought should be to improve the youth department. Can we help? Can it really be improved? Perhaps our involvement would make a major difference. But if things don't improve, perhaps we should look around for a sharper, more vital program. Many churches today have excellent youth programs, geared to both the spiritual and social needs of youth and often having a vital, soul-winning outreach. Involve your sons and daughters in this kind of program, especially in the peer-important teenage years.

Many other spiritual influences are apparent, and we'll briefly mention just a few. *All children need other Christian friends.* One of the most important dynamics of the Christian life is the fellow-ship, support, and encouragement of other Christian people. We should be alert to ways of making time for our children to play with Christian friends. This may mean a little effort on our part, but it will be worth a crosstown drive if they develop meaningful Christian friendships.

Christian literature and music also contribute to spiritual growth. Age-appropriate literature can do much to enlighten and encour-age growing Christian youth. Contemporary Christian magazines with solid content are published by many organizations like Cam-pus Crusade for Christ, Inter-Varsity, and Youth for Christ.[7] Some denominations also publish excellent materials for young people. Music is another channel for communicating Christian concepts; it can add an important cultural flavor to our homes and also cement certain spiritual truths. As we talk of literature and music, however, we don't mean to limit children to Christian information. Many high-quality secular books should be brought into Christian homes. These books bring a certain balance to our lives and keep us alert to the viewpoints of the world.

I personally believe every Christian parent should consider sending his children to Christian schools at some time in their training. Although I know children can be overprotected and sheltered in unhealthy ways, I feel the positive influences of Chris-tian friends and teachers usually offset this potential liability. As with all institutions, some Christian schools are good and some are not. Some are academically superior, while others struggle by with a half-qualified professional staff. Some schools are spiritually

[7] Campus Crusade for Christ, International, Arrowhead Springs, San Bernardino, CA 92414, publishes *Collegiate Challenge* and *Athletes in Action* magazines. Inter-Varsity Christian Fellowship, 233 Langdon, Madison, WI 53703, publishes *His* and *The Branch* magazines. Youth for Christ, International, P.O. Box 419, Wheaton, IL 60187, publishes *Campus Life* magazine.

alive, while some suffer from an ailment common to evangelical orthodoxy and are like the "frozen chosen." In my opinion, the effectiveness of most Christian elementary schools boils down to the influence of the principal and a few teachers. If these key people are creative and committed to a positive view of Christian living, they do much to encourage children along these paths.

This concludes our discussion of some basic elements of effective spiritual training. We see that we must begin with our relationships with our children. It is on this plane that they learn to feel accepted, gain confidence to communicate, and develop their emotional images of God. This healthy interaction needs to be accompanied by a family life-style that places Christ and Christian principles at its core. Not a day should pass without some conscious awareness of God's presence or divine intentions. And this kind of Christian experience must then be supplemented by formal instruction of a creative nature that makes Christian principles come alive in the language of our children.

APPLICATION

This chapter discusses three keys to Christian training. These are (1) the importance of the parent-child relationship to your children's image of God, (2) the importance of creative teaching, and (3) the importance of teaching spiritual truth from everyday life experiences.

EXERCISE I

Our children's image of God is the single most important element of spiritual training. Children learn about God both through the Scriptures and through our example. Our role as earthly parents provides the emotional basis for the intellectual knowledge of God gained through the Scriptures.

A. Compile a list of Scriptures describing the character and attributes of God. List these Scriptures below and the attributes they give of God. By looking in a concordance or Bible subject index under "God," you will find many of these Scriptures. As a starter, you might look up these verses: Psalms 90:2; 99:9; 139:1-6; Proverbs 5:21; Matthew 5:48; John 4:24; 17:3; 1 Corinthians 1:9; 10:13; 14:33; 1 Timothy 1:17; 1 John 1:5; 4:8.

	VERSE	ATTRIBUTE
1.	....	....
2.	....	....
3.	....	....
4.	....	....
5.	....	....
6.	....	....
7.	....	....
8.	....	....
9.	....	....
10.	....	....
11.	....	....
12.	....	....
13.	....	....
14.	....	....
15.	....	....
16.	....	....
17.	....	....
18.	....	....
19.	....	....
20.	....	....

You may teach your children about God's character by memorizing some of these verses as a family. Try taking a verse at one meal daily until the entire family has several of these verses and references well in mind.

B. You may also select biblical passages that illustrate God's character in dealing with the unsaved, His chosen people Israel, and sinning Christians. Select three biblical passages that illustrate important aspects of God's character. List the passages below, share them with your children, and write down the specific attributes or attitudes illustrated in each passage.

As a starter, you might use the story of Noah and the Flood in Chapters 6–9 of Genesis, the story of Joseph in Chapters 37–50 of Genesis, the prodigal son in Luke 15:11-32, or the woman taken in adultery in John 8:1-11. The Bible is full of similar concrete illustrations of God's dealings with man.

1. First passage ....

   Attributes demonstrated

   ....

   ....

   ....

   ....

   ....

2. Second passage ....

   Attributes demonstrated

   ....

   ....

   ....

. . . .

. . . .

3. Third passage . . . .

Attributes demonstrated

. . . .

. . . .

. . . .

. . . .

. . . .

How might you share these concepts with your children in a creative way that is appropriate to their age level?

. . . .

. . . .

. . . .

. . . .

. . . .

C. Children's emotional reactions to God are largely learned through their relationships with parents. Discuss with your mate the image of God and other authorities which your children are receiving through their relationships with you. Compare these attributes to those of God you just described.
1. List the positive attitudes your children are developing.

. . . .

. . . .

. . . .

. . . .

. . . .

2. List the negative attitudes they are learning.

. . . .

. . . .

. . . .

. . . .

. . . .

EXERCISE II

To help our children develop an integrated approach to the Christian life, we need to make a spiritual perspective central to our family life-style.

A. List and discuss with your mate three recent times you have used a common daily occurrence to teach a spiritual truth.

1. . . . .

2. . . . .

3. . . . .

B. Thinking back over the last two or three days, list three times you have let situations go by which could have been used to teach some important spiritual concepts.

1. . . . .

2. . . . .

3. . . . .

C. List and briefly discuss a significant spiritual lesson you personally have learned through some life experience in the past six months.

. . . .

. . . .

. . . .

. . . .

D. Pick an article from today's newspaper and think about its spiritual implications. What lesson may your family be reminded of from it?

. . . .

. . . .

. . . .

. . . .

CHAPTER FOUR

YOUR CHILD'S CONSCIENCE — BIRTH TO ADOLESCENCE

Conscience is the part of personality that evaluates behavior. It measures our attitudes and actions by a standard and therefore helps to guide our lives. If our children are to adopt and maintain a biblical set of values, they must have healthy consciences.

The Bible mentions three general types of conscience. The first is a *good conscience.* People with good consciences have a proper set of values and are living according to these inner moral guides. 1 Peter 3:16 says, "Having a good conscience; that, whereas they speak evil of you, as of evildoers, they may be ashamed that falsely accuse your good conversation in Christ." In other words, a person with a good conscience has a biblical set of values and lives up to these inner guides. When another person tries to condemn him, the accuser ends up feeling ashamed because he realizes he has judged an upright person wrongfully.

Other people seem to have a *deadened conscience.* For some reason they can commit sinful actions without much sense of wrong. In the extreme, this type of conscience is represented in the criminal, the swindler, or the so-called psychopath. These people have such deadened or undeveloped moral standards that they have little sense of responsibility or concern for others; they do as they please as long as they aren't caught. 1 Timothy 1:19 says, "Holding faith, and a good conscience; which some having put away concerning faith have made shipwreck."

Some other people have a *weak conscience*. This third type of conscience is alluded to in 1 Corinthians 8:12. In that passage Paul writes, "But when ye sin so against the brethren, and wound their weak conscience, ye sin against Christ." These Christian brethren had overly strict consciences. They felt condemned for doing innocent things like eating meat; they didn't understand there was nothing innately sinful in this act. Because of faulty childhood experiences, many people have developed such harsh, condemning consciences. They continually deprive themselves of fulfilling life experiences in a masochistic sort of way; each desire for pleasure is accompanied by a morbid guilt emotion. They feel "I shouldn't do that" or "I don't deserve the pleasure." Even minor transgressions are followed by severe feelings of guilt that lead to depression and despair.

Putting these passages together, we see that a conscience may be too loose and allow sinful attitudes and actions. It may also be too harsh and prohibit enjoyment of many good things. Or, it may awaken us to potentially sinful attitudes and actions and enable us to guide our behavior properly.

The concerned parent tries to reach a balance. He asks, "How can I teach my children lasting spiritual and moral values without instilling a punitive condemning conscience?" Three contemporary authors have summarized the problem this way:

> Uncertain as we may be about the optimal average, however, we can say something about the extremes of conscience and its lack. The child with too strong a conscience is guilt ridden. His own impulses constantly excite him to confession and to a too instant admission of wrongdoing. He is prevented from experimentation with new impulses; he dares not risk the danger of self punishment. New ideas and new experiences, even new people, are dangerous to him. He becomes rigid and inflexible in his judgments of others, a purveyor of sanctimony and propriety. His repressed hostilities are brought into the service of his moral judgments. In childhood he is a prig, a teacher's pet; in adulthood he can become cruel and vicious in his expression of moral indignation. Worst of all, perhaps, he can have no fun in life, for fun itself is subject to inner control.
>
> At the other extreme is the child with a weak conscience. What he lacks in guilt he makes up in fear. His actions are bounded only by the possibility of his being caught and punished for his wrongdoings. His moral judgments are based on expediency. He cannot be trusted out of sight and supervision.

His infantile impulses remain strong, and in the absence of a punitive disciplinarian he has no reluctance to express them. He may bully younger or weaker children, steal and lie if he thinks he can get away with it, and flees to hide when anything happens that may conceivably be viewed amiss by adults. In childhood he is aggressive and mean, a troublemaker at home and at school. In adulthood, he may be a conscienceless rogue in his social and business relationships, an undisciplinable bum or a criminal.[1]

This well-phrased summary expresses a vital truth. Children need to develop a healthy conscience. They need a set of guiding principles and a meaningful philosophy of life. At the same time they need a freedom and flexibility that allows for individuality and spontaneous self-expression.

To help our children in their growth, this chapter takes a deeper look at the true meaning of conscience and its makeup. We will try to answer the questions, "*What* makes up the conscience?" and "*How* does the conscienceless infant gradually learn a set of internal moral guidelines?" Following chapters will attempt to show how the Christian parent can help his children develop well-balanced consciences and a set of biblical inner values.

Like all human attributes, the conscience does not spring into full bloom at some specific stage of life. The amoral infant with his great potential for both good and evil does not suddenly become spiritually mature or moral at the age of 6, 13, 18, or even 21. Instead, like all other personal attributes, the conscience develops gradually. Over a period of years the unknowing infant gradually gains the intellectual and social ability to develop a system of inner values and controls. This chapter describes some of the essential elements of this growth process.

To clarify our thinking we will break up this development process into five basic stages. Although these stages overlap, they describe important steps in the journey toward mature morality. They can also give us insight into the kinds of parental guidance that promote our children's moral growth.

STAGE ONE: MORALITY OF PHYSICAL RESTRAINT

During the first year of life children show practically no signs

[1] From pp. 391-392 in *Patterns of Child Rearing* by Robert R. Sears, Eleanor E. Maccoby and Harry Levin. Copyright © 1957 by Harper & Row, Publishers, Inc. By permission of the publishers.

69

of conscience. They need constant supervision. When they have a desire they try immediately to fulfill it. The light of a fire attracts them much as flame does a moth; they crawl slowly toward it and may reach out unless they are restrained. Similarly, a dangerous piece of glass or the jagged edge of an opened can may harm a child unless he is removed from its presence. In these early months the center of control is completely outside the infant. He has no personal controls. Because of this, the first forerunner of conscience might be called a *morality of physical restraint*.

STAGE TWO: FEAR AND RESPECT

Toward the end of the first year of life and especially during the second, children begin to show the first signs of a developing conscience. After a few spankings a child reaches out for a knick-knack on his mother's shelf. Then, remembering the last time he reached for mother's property and the consequence of that action, he withdraws his hand and moves on. Another child touches a hot stove and quickly withdraws his hand; he learns not to touch the stove because of the hurtful consequence. These common happenings illustrate the second stage of conscience development, a stage that might be called *the morality of fear and respect of consequences*.

This stage has two related sides, both involving the capacity of children to remember the consequences of their actions. The first dynamic is the principle of fear. When a child is severely punished or threatened, he reacts with strong emotions. Whether he outwardly shows it or not, he experiences uncomfortable feelings of anxiety. Fearing future *external* punishment, he may conform to avoid the threatened discipline.

The other dynamic of this second moral stage takes a slightly different twist. This is the concept of respect. When a child touches a hot stove he learns respect for the consequences of his actions. There is no fear of a punishing authority; no one is going to try to get even with him for his misbehavior. Instead, there is an *internal* awareness of good reasons for avoiding some activities.

To illustrate the differences between fear and respect, let's take a practical parental problem. All of us want our children to be careful as they cross the street. We can go about this two ways. We may yell, "Look out! Here comes a car!" upon approaching

70

every street. This is a fear motive — it creates strong anxiety in the child and makes him nervous each time he nears a moving car. In contrast, we may say calmly but firmly, "When we cross the street, we look in both directions. We don't want to get in the way of a moving car." This is motivating from respect of consequences — under this system children learn respect of traffic without developing an unhealthy anxiety.

Three Elements of Fear

This distinction is important. The fear dynamic has three negative elements. In the first place, the anxiety is usually very strong. This is unfortunate, since strong anxiety actually interferes with personal performance and adjustment. A child who conforms out of fear is an anxious, careful, neurotic person. By contrast, the anxiety associated with a healthy respect of potentially harmful consequences is not severe. It serves more as a warning signal than as a panic reaction.

A second difference between fear and respect lies in the cause of the anxiety. In fear motivation, the anxiety is not over the misbehavior; rather it is over the fear of being caught and punished. This means that the motivation for behavior is the fear of punishment, not the knowledge of negative consequences of behavior.

Finally, fear motivation differs from the respect of consequences in terms of the source of control. In fear motivation, the source of control is external to the person. He doesn't conform out of a desire for respectful, mutual relationships; instead, he conforms so he won't be caught and punished. If he felt he could get away with it, he would continue to misbehave. In respect of consequences, the seat of the control lies within the person. He behaves out of respect for potentially negative consequences or out of concern for others rather than to avoid his parents' punishments. This is a more mature morality.

This briefly summarizes the nature of the second stage of moral development. There is a healthy dynamic that leads to a mature morality — respect for the natural consequences of misbehavior. There is also a negative motivation which often takes precedence over the first — the unhealthy dynamic of fear. In this children learn to behave to avoid punishment. The seat of this morality is external and based upon a threat. Although this motive may lead to good behavior, it does so out of fear and may bring about neurotic complications.

STAGE THREE: INTERNALIZED PARENT

From ages two to five, other things are happening. A child's intelligence rapidly expands. He begins to understand new concepts and ideas. He becomes more competent and gains a greater sense of self-respect. At the same time he develops peer relations; as he nears school age, he interacts with several "friends." For the first time he has to learn to give and take. Although we sometimes "wonder if they'll ever learn," children slowly gain a respect for other people and a willingness to share. This is another seed in the development of conscience. It is an important element of the later-developing ability to emphasize with others.

During this period children are aware of feeling small and weak. They know they cannot overpower their parents, older siblings, or bigger playmates. To overcome this feeling of weakness, children turn toward their parents. They know the parents are strong, and they hope to gain a sense of strength from them. We have all heard children make comments like "My dad can lick your dad" or "My mother cooks better than your mother." These childish challenges reflect the attempts of small children to gain a sense of strength and superiority by identifying with a strong or successful parent.

Both consciously and unconsciously, children want to be like their mothers and fathers. This process is known as identification or internalization. In it children gradually take on their parents' attitudes and values; they become increasingly like their parents. They find that by obeying parents and mimicking them they gain parental approval and support. They also hope that by imitating parents they will soon become big and strong like them. They mimic parental mannerisms, pick up their style of speech, and adopt many of their attitudes. This process is the major source of the development of conscience.

As a part of this process of identification, a third stage of morality comes into play. This may be called *the morality of the internalized parent*. We learn attitudes as well as actions from our parents. A boy may be seen trying on his father's shoes and clomping down the hall. A young girl playing house may be heard to say to her doll, "No! No! Mommy will have to spank you!" In both thoughts and actions, children take on parents' values.

The Ideal Self

As in the second stage of fear and respect, the level of the internalized parent also has two elements. One is positive and the other negative. The first kind of identification is based on love and healthy idolization of the parent. The young girl loves her mother and wants to be like her; she puts on her mother's long dress, finds an oversized purse and "plays house." Similarly, boys adopt their father's attitudes. If his father complains each time he removes the trash or works in the yard, his son soon may be heard echoing the complaint. On the other hand, if Dad enjoys his outdoor work, the son will look forward to these times.

In the moral realm the same principle is in operation. When parents show a deep concern and respect for others, children soon learn this attitude. When parents make their Christian faith a vital part of family living, children soon may be heard praying, singing, and showing other spiritual interests.

Out of these experiences children develop an image of who and how they think they ought to be. This *ideal self*, as it is known, consists of all the values learned early in life. It may include "being a nice boy," being intelligent, being strong and athletic, being beautiful, or being Christian. In short, it consists of all the attitudes, thoughts, actions, and ideals that children take in from their parents. By adolescence this ideal self or "ego ideal" is well formed. While new ideals may be added, the basic content and attitudes are firmly entrenched; this ego ideal will serve as a measuring rod throughout the rest of life. All of our later adult thoughts and actions are judged by how well they line up to these ideals.

It's easy to see the importance of this ideal self. If it is too low, children will never be motivated to reach for higher things. On the other hand, if it is too high and unrealistic, they will be doomed to repeated failure and feelings of frustration. One of the important tasks of parents is to help children develop a good, but realistic, ideal self.

73

The Corrective Self

This ideal self is only one side of the internalization process. Children internalize not only their parents' ideals, but also their parents' attitudes toward misbehavior and their methods of discipline. Just as children develop an ideal concept of what they think they should become (their ideal self), they also adopt their parents' disciplinary or corrective patterns as their own. Just as the ideal self is largely crystallized by adolescence, this *corrective self* is well set in the early years of life. Even after children grow up and leave their parents *they tend to try to correct themselves in the same manner as their parents.* If parents have repeatedly said, "Shame on you," "What's wrong with you?" or "That's stupid," children later react to their own failings with similar thoughts. If parents have become angry or subtly implied "We love you less when you are bad," children will later get angry at themselves or feel unworthy of others' love when they misbehave.

We must ask ourselves, "What happens to a child who fails to live up to the ideals of his parents and other significant authorities

(his internalized ideal self)?" The answer lies in the way his parents react to his misbehavior; each kind of parental response determines what corrective patterns the child will choose for himself. There are six options; in brief, a parent may

(1) punish the child,
(2) shame the child for his failure,
(3) subtly reject the child by being angry at him for the misbehavior,
(4) ignore the failure, or let the child profit from the consequences of his actions,
(5) lovingly accept the child and help him grow toward maturity, or
(6) help the child develop a more realistic standard.

All these reactions are equally important. Let's discuss in this chapter the first three options, the negative ones. They are the source of all later neurotic guilt emotions.

Children quickly learn to expect certain parental reactions when they misbehave. Take punishment for example. Children are told, "Since you did that you must be punished." In other words, each time they fall short of an expected standard *they learn to expect punishment.* They develop a "balanced scale" concept. The idea is this: "I need to go through life free from anxiety and fear of punishment [that is, with a clear conscience]. But I sometimes sin or fall short of others' expectations. When this happens, I deserve punishment. Until that punishment comes, I feel anxious. Once my punishment has come I am again relieved; I have paid my debts and can operate without fear." Unless this type of child is punished, he continues to experience anxiety, since the threat of punishment is hanging over him. Once the punishment comes, he feels he has atoned for his misdeeds and is relieved of his anxiety. Diagramatically the process looks like this.

As children grow up, a problem occurs. Since parents are no longer constantly around to punish for misbehaviors, how may their anxiety be alleviated? The long history of conditioning has deeply ingrained the attitude, "When you do wrong you must be punished." Even in the parents' absence this nagging fear persists. To relieve this anxiety children begin to inflict punishment on themselves. Children may sometimes be observed playing parent to themselves; they say "No, No, Johnny" and gently spank their

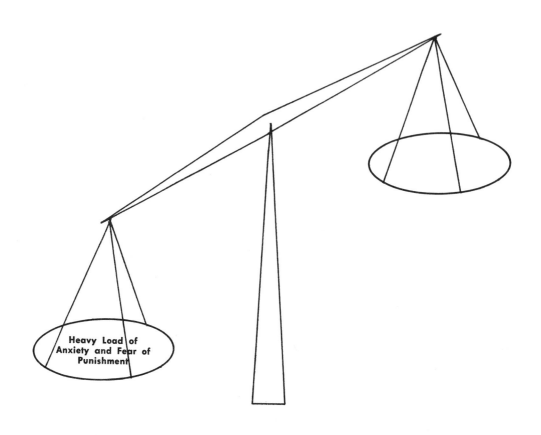

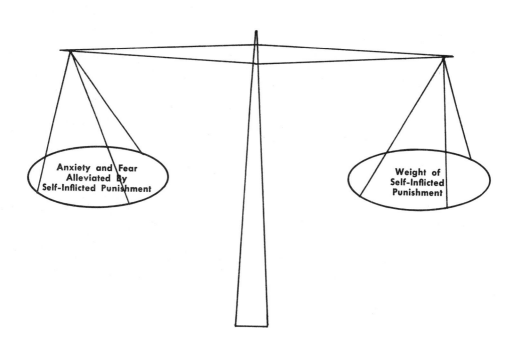

own wrists. As adults we all continue this process of self-atonement. In the absence of parents or of punishing others we develop intricate ways of inflicting punishment on ourselves.

A client of mine routinely cut herself with razor blades as a self-inflicted punishment. This girl had deep feelings of guilt over sexual behavior. The self-inflicted pain gave her temporary relief from feelings of guilt and also gave a distorted sexual pleasure through a masochistic dynamic.

Most of us don't turn to such obvious physical forms of punishment. Instead, we substitute a mental pain or an expectation of punishment for an actual self-inflicted pain. This psychical pain takes the form of a threat. It says, "You misbehaved. You shouldn't act that way. Sometime you're going to get caught and really get it."

Some people project this punitive process onto God. They feel "somehow, somewhere, God is going to get even." Take the Judgment Seat of Christ, for example. What is your immediate reaction to the thought? Apprehension? Do you have a vague feeling that then you will be found out? Many people do. They respond to this with thoughts of fear, anxiety, and shame. In other words, they are living under the constant expectation of divine judgment for misdeeds.

Other people fear God will punish them by involving them in an accident or illness. Still others fear they may give birth to a deformed child or undergo some unusual suffering. All these fears come about from the process of internalization. They consist of the internalized voice of parents which continues to operate even after children have left their homes.

A person may ask, "Why do we keep expecting punishment after we are grown?" or "It seems as if we would outgrow this fear and guilt motivation learned from our parents." These are good questions and important to our understanding. Both the ideal self and the corrective self (the disciplinary procedures of parents) become deeply embedded in our thinking processes. Although there are some complex psychological reasons for this, let me give a simple illustration. We all have picked up some phrases and voice inflections from our parents. Most of us have retained other of their habits. In disciplining our own children, for example, we often use the same words, tone of voice, or methods of punishment that our parents used on us. Let's say we started today to over-come these habits. We vow never to use the same expressions as our parents, alter our tone of voice, reject their social and political standards, and use completely different disciplinary methods with our children. Needless to say, this would be an impossible task; what changes we might make would come slowly. The deeply ingrained patterns of our life are strongly resistant to change, even as mature adults. We must always keep this principle in mind. The attitudes our children learn toward themselves and life are going to be hard to alter later on.

A second type of parental response to misbehavior is to *impart a sense of shame or self-depreciation*. Haven't all of us at one time or another said to our children, "Shame on you. You know better than that"? Or, even more strongly, we reprimand them with the statement, "Look how you have let us down. After all we've done for you, you have to hurt us this way!" Excessive use of verbal punishment can become a basic cause of depression and loss of self-esteem. Even though we are trying to instill Christian virtues, this form of motivation may cause serious maladjustments in our children. Repeated messages of "You should do better," "What's wrong with you?" or "You know better than that" become im-bedded in the personality.

Even after they are grown, our children maintain this same type of self-esteem. In the physical absence of their parents they keep on saying, "Shame on you. You're a bad person." This self-depreciation is one of the main dynamics of discouragement and depression.

A third type of parental response to misbehavior is a *veiled threat of personal rejection*. All of us sometime have been on the receiving end of a loved one's anger. Parents, siblings, peers, or admired teachers reacted to our misconduct, not with loving con-cern, but with anger and frustration. Similarly, some parents ventilate their hostile feelings on their children. This can be done through a harsh word, a hard spanking, or an angry look. Under extreme duress some parents even yell, "I hate you!" or "Get out of my sight!" Parents find that all these reactions may frighten children into good behavior. Faced with the consequence of losing parental love, most children try to change their behavior to please the ones they love. But to a growing child even an unfounded fear of punishment instills a deep fear of rejection. He thinks, "When I do wrong my parents get angry. They send me to my room or spank me hard. They probably don't love me!"

A woman told me she had great difficulty controlling her newly adopted daughter. She had tried everything and finally found a way that worked. "I tell her," she said proudly, "God doesn't love you when you're naughty!" Sensing the deep rejection the child must feel, I asked the lady, "Does God love you when you are naughty?" Then she got the point. Think of it — to instill in an impressionable child the inner fear that "God doesn't love you when you're naughty"! But each of us is all too human. We all have experiences through which we communicate "People love you less when you are naughty." No matter how many times we tell our children "We love you just the way you are," our parental anger and frustrations undermine these messages.

This concludes our summary of one side of the disciplinary picture. We may motivate our children out of fear of punishment, threats of loss of love, or attacks on their self-esteem. Each of these three methods is internalized and forms part of our children's consciences, their corrective self. In adulthood these will have negative consequences. They will lead to anxiety, depression, and neurotic guilt emotions. This is the negative side of the process of internalization. By taking in the punitive, threatening, and hostile portions of parental attitudes, children are programmed for later feelings of depression and neurotic guilt. Each time they fall short of their ideal self they will automatically trigger this corrective self. The emotion triggered by this corrective self is guilt. But this form of guilt is not a healthy warning light — instead, it is an inhibiting, oppressive guilt emotion.

Fortunately, all forms of discipline are not so potentially damaging. As a matter of fact, proper parental attitudes may play a major role in helping children develop both a healthy self-esteem and a biblical set of values. Chapter five will deal with the disciplinary attitudes that lead to a mature morality and a healthy corrective self. God's discipline of us as His sons will serve as our model for that discussion.

(The application exercises for this chapter are at the end of chapter five. You may do them now, or you may want to perform all the exercises after completing the discussion of the conscience in the next chapter. If you wish to do them now, exercises I and III are applicable.)

YOUR CHILD'S CONSCIENCE — ADOLESCENCE TO MATURITY

Now that we have surveyed the process of identification, let's take a summary look at moral development during the third stage of life (from about three to eleven years of age). What causes children to be moral during this stage? There remains, of course, the morality of fear and respect from level two. And there is also a developing sensitivity to the needs of others. But the strongest influence of this period is the process of identification. Children largely adopt the values of their parents. Have you ever heard the eight-year-old child of two Republican parents say seriously, "I'm a Democrat"? Or have you ever heard the nine-year-old daughter of Baptist parents say, "I'm a Catholic"? Of course not! These political and religious beliefs reflect children's identification with their parents. For some children, this identification consists of proper and realistic ideals coupled with sensitive, loving disciplinary methods. For others, the parental standards are excessively low or high, and the disciplinary methods are punitive or nonexistent.

THE LIMITS OF CHILDISH MORALITY

As you can see, each of the first three types of morality leaves much to be desired. They are necessary steps in the progressive development of conscience, but they are not mature processes. Physical restraint is necessary for young children but requires the

81

continual presence of an authority. An adult who does good only when physically forced by others is obviously a maladjusted person.

Fear of punishment may have a small place in the moral development of young children. But what if this were as far as conscience developed? If there were no fear of being caught, people would continue to misbehave. Unfortunately, nearly all of us have some remnants of this stage of moral development. If we are pretty sure no patrolman is near, we gradually ease the speedometer five or ten miles above the limit. In more blatant forms, people who cheat on expense accounts and income taxes reflect this same level of morality. As long as they don't get caught, they continue on their way.

The second aspect of level two, the awareness of negative consequences of our behavior, is a good lesson that applies throughout a lifetime. All mature adults refrain from some actions because they know they would bring about painful consequences.

The third level of morality, that of the internalized parent, is a step better than the previous. Even in the absence of authority we continue to behave. To the degree that we have internalized the values of loving, mature parents this type of morality is very good. Throughout life each of us consciously and unconsciously patterns ourselves after admired and respected individuals. But this level has its weaknesses, too. To the degree that we have internalized the fear of punishment and the guilt dynamic that forces us to punish ourselves in our parents' absence, the motive for moral behavior remains self-centered. We refrain from stealing, for example, but not out of a concern for others and a respect for their property. Instead, we act properly because we feel anxious or guilty if we don't. This type of morality also has another drawback: the self-punishment often leads to depression and a low self-image.

The level of the internalized parent has one final drawback: it is an inherited morality, not a chosen one. Although we hope our children will adopt most of our parental values, we must realize they need to come to these standards in part by their own experience. Otherwise, their values are simply a parroting of our own, and they will have no personal deep commitment to their standards.

STAGE FOUR: THE ADOLESCENT CONSCIENCE

During adolescence a conscience crisis occurs. Under the impact of increased intellectual ability, greater physical maturity, an enlarged world view, and, most of all, peer pressures, the teenager begins to reevaluate his standards.

When the adolescent begins to think for himself, he sees the biased rigidity of some of his parents' standards. As he searches for his identity, he also feels compelled to assert his independence from his parents. Some of this is good. If the adolescent never learns to think for himself, he will always be a "yes-man." His values and ideals will never be his own; he will simply be a puppet of his parents.

As a part of finding his own identity, the typical teenager rethinks some of his morality. He outwardly rebels against a few of his parents' values just to see if he can get away with it. He is trying to separate himself both from his parents and from their internalized ideals.

The sensitive parent is ready for this challenge. Instead of vainly struggling to keep his teenager at an immature internalized or fear-based level of morality, he encourages this newfound search for personal values and identity. He allows the teenager to think for himself but in an open way discusses the reasons for supporting a biblical morality. Sometimes this process is difficult for us as parents; we have invested a great deal of energy in our value systems, and we react to any questioning of it. This plays into the hands of the growing adolescent. Whenever he upsets us, he feels he is strong; he knows he has won a victory. His time of feeling weak is passed; he now has the power to upset us. This is an unfortunate occurrence.

The wise parent is flexible. He is willing to reevaluate his own morality. He may see that some of his taboos and values are not specifically mentioned in the Scriptures. While there may be good personal reasons for avoiding or endorsing these extra-biblical attitudes, the sensitive parent does not claim the power of divine inspiration to force his adolescent into conformity. Instead, he majors in biblical principles and non-defensively gives his personal reasons for his unique brand of morality. At the same time, he gradually allows his teenager to assume greater responsibility in determining a personal set of values.

Although this process may seem frightening, it is essential to mature morality. If we are convinced of the accuracy of the Bible and the ministry of the Holy Spirit, we will be willing to let God lead our teenagers into His truth without coercion. We will lead. We will listen. We will quietly discuss. But we will not condemn, coerce, or angrily try to force our values on our children. This process obviously requires good parent-teen communication, but it is perhaps the most crucial element of our growing children's developing morality.

STAGE FIVE: MATURE CONSCIENCE

The mature conscience should be operating well by late adolescence and early adulthood. Hypothetically, this conscience should be entirely free of the necessity of external controls and restraint. The mature person does not need to be motivatd by the fear of others or by an inner sense of self-punishment. Instead, he judges each situation on the basis of its merits. He considers the positive and negative consequences of his actions to himself and others. He refrains from stealing, for example, not from the fear of being caught or feeling guilty — these motivations are self-centered. Instead, he refrains from stealing because he recognizes the rights of others and their property.

The mature person acts morally, not out of coercion or seeking to avoid punishment and guilt, but because he has a genuine concern for others. As God's sons we should have the same motives. As Christians we are not motivated to obey God to avoid punishment; Christ has already paid for all our sins. And we shouldn't be motivated merely to remove our own guilty feelings — this is selfish. Instead, we follow God's commandments out of love and a desire to do the helpful thing for ourselves, the cause of Christ, and other people.[1]

At this point another factor enters the picture. We are not left merely to our own judgments about the rightfulness of an action. As Christians we are aware of a number of divine absolutes in the

---

[1] John 13:34, "And so I am giving a new commandment to you now — love each other just as much as I love you" (*Living Bible*).

John 14:15, "If you love me, obey Me" (*Living Bible*).

1 John 3:16, "We know what real love is from Christ's example in dying for us. And so we also ought to lay down our lives for our Christian brothers" (*Living Bible*).

area of personal living. What is to be our stand in these areas? Does the mature person immediately say yes to every biblical standard without giving serious consideration to the purpose of divine teachings? Or, on the other hand, is the mature person the one who doggedly questions every authoritative statement of God or any other authority? Actually, neither of these extremes is healthy or mature.

The person who immediately conforms to every authoritative comment is usually a dependent or fear-oriented person. Lacking a sense of individuality and self-confidence, he is afraid to question. At first glance he may seem mature because of his "faith." But an unquestioning faith that fails to ask "why?" is actually naive. While biblical standards are absolute and authoritative, they do have sound logic behind them. God does not simply say, "Do this because I say so!" Instead, He points out that His commands are actually for our own good, or for the good of other people. He doesn't expect us to blindly follow all His guidelines. Instead, He wants us to be sensitive to the needs of others and to follow His guidance out of love. People who passively accept all authoritative truth are actually stuck at one of the childish dependent stages of morality.

On the other hand, some people think they are "mature" because they accept nothing without doubting. These people pride themselves on their intellect and their sophistication. They accept a biblical standard only when it conforms to their logic. They rebel against authority and try desperately to develop a sense of individuality by refusing to accept any authority beyond their own. In other words, they reject all authority and become their own judge. This frail attempt at building self-esteem is a far cry from personal maturity.

The mature person combines these seemingly opposing traits. He is able both to accept authority and to think for himself. Because he has recognized the value of authority, he is willing to follow it. In the case of a Christian, he is convinced of the accuracy of the Bible and its pronouncements in moral areas. When he comes to a statement contrary to his own opinion, he thinks, "I wonder why that is? From my perspective it doesn't seem necessary. But I have experienced the new birth and God's faithfulness, and I know it must be for our benefit. I will try to understand

Step	Type of Control	Advantages	Disadvantages	Appropriate Age
I	Physical Restraint	(1) Protects young child from physical dangers.	(1) Requires constant supervision.	Birth — 1 year with occasional restraints later, but diminishing to nearly nothing.
IIA	Punishment and Fear of an External Authority	(1) Protects child from dangers. (2) Begins to teach child right and wrong. (3) Protects rights and property of others.	(1) Punishment requires continual presence of authority. (2) Punishment must be severe and frequent to maintain standards. (3) Punishment causes dependency and hostility. (4) Motive for morality is self-centered (to avoid punishment).	9 months — 4 or 5 years with great lessening of direct parental intervention in physical discipline or force after this time.
IIB	Respect of Consequences	(1) Teaches negative consequences of some behavior without parental force or fear motivation.		Throughout life.
III	Internalized Parent	(1) Protects rights and property of others. (2) Protects self from consequences of negative actions. (3) Doesn't require continual presence of an authority. (4) Teaches socialized responses such as manners and neatness.	(1) Motive for morality is self-centered to the degree that the internalization is of fear and guilt. (2) Morality tends to be rigid and limited to that taught by parents and other significant authorities. (3) May be associated with a	2 or 3 years — adolescence. This process occurs through all of life but is especially prominent in the first 10 or 12 years.

			Adolescence
	(5) Leads to good self-image to the degree that the internalization is of a loving, accepting parent.	condemning attitude toward others who violate one's standards. (4) Self-punishment raises anxiety and depression and lowers self-esteem.	
IV Adolescent	(1) Helps morality become the child's own chosen one rather than simply an imitation of his parents. (2) Broadens and creates a more sensitive morality.	(1) May involve temporary rebellion.	
V Mature Morality	(1) Protects rights and privileges of others. (2) Protects self from consequences of one's own negative actions. (3) Doesn't require presence of an authority. (4) Maintains mature consideration of others. (5) Maintains a flexible, sensitive (but not condemning) conscience showing concern for self and others. (6) Maintains healthy self-image and a sense of individuality.		

why, but if I don't I will accept it as important even though I don't understand its purpose now."

This summarizes our concept of the goal of maturity in conscience. People with mature consciences can:

1. Respect the rights and privileges of others because they have a sense of warmth, empathy, and concern.
2. See the consequences of behavior for both self and others, and act according to those implications.
3. Respect authority and learn from the guidance of others.
4. Think independently and rationally, not bound on the one hand by inner fears of punishment or a sense of guilt, or on the other hand by a rebellious attitude which rejects all authority but one's own.
5. Accept divine absolutes and the leading of the Holy Spirit while seeking to understand their implications and continuing to accept them, even when they diverge from our reasoning.
6. Make all their moral decisions out of a mature love for God, themselves, and others.

This table summarizes the five stages of conscience development. All these stages have some influence through life, but we should be moving toward the mature morality of level five.

APPLICATION

Chapters four and five give an overview of moral development by breaking down the growth of conscience into five stages. Although moral growth is on a continuum and each stage overlaps the others to some degree, this breakdown may provide greater understanding of the nature of moral growth and the parental attitudes and actions that foster healthy moral growth.

EXERCISE I

Chapter four indicates that a person's conscience may be either too lenient, too harsh, or well balanced. Discuss and answer the following questions to clarify the importance of this concept.

A. What problems will a person with a lenient or deadened conscience likely have?

. . . .

. . . .

. . . .

B. What do you think causes some people to develop this type of morality?

. . . .

. . . .

. . . .

C. What problems will a person with an overly strict conscience probably develop?

. . . .

. . . .

. . . .

D. What do you think causes some people to develop this type of weak conscience?

. . . .

. . . .

. . . .

E. What is the advantage of having a healthy conscience?

. . . .

. . . .

. . . .

F. What parental attitudes and actions promote this kind of moral growth?

. . . .

. . . .

. . . .

What stage of morality is being taught by each of the following parental comments or actions? The correct answers are given at the end of this application section. You will notice that some comments reflect more than one level of morality and that stages two, three and four each have positive sides (respect of consequences, identification with a loving parent, and a search to accept values as one's own) as well as negative sides (fear, identification with a punitive parent, and rebellion).

1. Saying loudly, "Stop that right now or you'll be spanked!" ....
2. Asking, "What do you think we should do here, John?" ....
3. Holding a child and physically barring him from some activity. ....
4. Allowing two children to finish a physical fight. ....
5. Repeatedly asking a child, "Do you think you should do that?" or "Be careful, honey, you might get hurt." ....
6. Discussing with a young person, "What will happen if we do this?" ....
7. Saying, "God will have to punish you if you're naughty." Or singing, "You'd better watch out, ... you'd better not pout, ... Santa Claus is coming to town. ..." ....
8. Being flexible and open to the suggestions of others. ....
9. Becoming angry with children when they disobey. ....
10. Tithing, witnessing, and being regularly involved in Christian work. ....

EXERCISE III

A. Discuss with your mate and list a number of elements of your ideal self. This should include attitudes, actions, and aspirations, whether they seem big or small. They may include things like being a straight-A student, having a spotless house, financial success, never losing your temper, being very sociable, among others.

1. ....

2. ....

3. ....

4. ....

5. ....

6. ....

7. ....

8. ....

9. ....

10. ....

B. We all have a corrective self. In other words, when we fall short of the demands of our ideal self, we try to discipline ourselves in order to change. List two times recently when you have sinned or fallen short of your standards. Your answers to the following questions will help clarify the concept of the internalized parent.

First Problem: ....

....

1. How did you try to correct yourself? ....

....

....

2. Is your internalized corrective attitude a loving, patient,

accepting one, or is it scolding, demanding, or impatient?

. . . .

3. Do you see remnants of your parents in your corrective

attitude toward yourself? . . . . If so, how? . . . .

. . . .

SECOND PROBLEM: . . . .

. . . .

1. How did you try to correct yourself? . . . .

. . . .

. . . .

2. Is your internalized corrective attitude a loving, patient, accepting one, or is it scolding, demanding, or impatient?

. . . .

3. Do you see remnants of your parents in your corrective

attitude toward yourself? . . . . If so, how? . . . .

. . . .

EXERCISE IV

A. Discuss two disciplinary settings or two recent times of communication for each of your children. List the problem and your attempt at instruction or discipline. Then tell which stage of morality you were promoting.

FIRST CHILD

FIRST PROBLEM: . . . .

....

1. Discipline or instruction: ....

....

2. Stage of morality the discipline or instruction promoted:

....

SECOND PROBLEM: ....

....

1. Discipline or instruction: ....

....

2. Stage of morality the discipline or instruction promoted:

....

SECOND CHILD

FIRST PROBLEM: ....

....

1. Discipline or instruction: ....

....

2. Stage of morality the discipline or instruction promoted:

....

SECOND PROBLEM: ....

....

1. Discipline or instruction: ....

....

2. Stage of morality the discipline or instruction promoted:

....

THIRD CHILD

FIRST PROBLEM: ....

....

1. Discipline or instruction: ....

....

2. Stage of morality the discipline or instruction promoted:

....

SECOND PROBLEM: ....

....

1. Discipline or instruction: ....

....

2. Stage of morality the discipline or instruction promoted:

....

B. If you were promoting an immature level of moral development, what could you have done differently in each instance?

FIRST CHILD

FIRST PROBLEM: ....

. . . .

SECOND PROBLEM: . . . .

. . . .

SECOND CHILD

FIRST PROBLEM: . . . .

. . . .

SECOND PROBLEM: . . . .

. . . .

THIRD CHILD

FIRST PROBLEM: . . . .

. . . .

SECOND PROBLEM: . . . .

. . . .

ANSWER KEY FOR EXERCISE II
1. Level 2 (Fear)
2. Level 4 or 5
3. Level 1
4. Level 2 (Respect of Consequences)
5. Level 2 (Fear) or 3
6. Level 2 (Respect of Consequences) and 4 and 5
7. Level 3 (Internalizing a punitive parent)
8. Level 3 (Identification)
9. Level 3 (Internalizing a punitive parent)
10. Level 3 (Internalizing a good parent)

CHAPTER SIX

ROADBLOCKS TO MORALITY

Our brief sketch of the course of moral development of children leads naturally to the question, "What can the average parent do to help his child move toward the mature morality of level five?" It's one thing to see a desired pattern of moral growth, but quite another to put this pattern into action! In this chapter we will take a look at some attitudes and actions that inhibit healthy moral growth and unknowingly fixate our children on the first four levels of immature morality.

Before turning to specific parental attitudes, we should point out that the most basic ingredient of all effective child rearing is the adjustment of the parents. Specific techniques of discipline are not nearly so important as our attitudes. Take spanking for example. Some parents feel spankings are old-fashioned and cruel; they never physically discipline their children. They do, however, often lose their tempers with their offspring. The anxiety caused by this parental anger is potentially much more harmful than a good physical spanking done in love! It is the attitude that counts.

THE PERMISSIVE PARENT

The first inadequate attitude toward rearing children is permissiveness. During the 1940s a new wave swept the child-rearing and educational practices of American culture. Under the names of progressive education, democracy, and child-centered homes, this movement touched nearly every corner of society. Well-known

97

educators and psychologists expounded the virtues of a permissive attitude toward children. Men like John Dewey in education, Carl Rogers in psychology, and Benjamin Spock in pediatrics were outspoken leaders of this movement. They attacked the inhibiting effects of the so-called authoritarian attitude and offered a child-centered emphasis in its place.

At the core of this new attitude was the belief that children could make their own choices and direct their own lives with very little outside interference. Underlying this notion was the philosophical belief that man is basically good and has the capabilities to direct his own existence. This belief obviously led to a negative view toward authority. If children could make effective decisions on their own, there was little need for parental authority. As a matter of fact, authority was seen as squelching the child's inner growth to actualization.

One of the most extreme statements of this position was given by the author of the controversial *Summerhill*. A. S. Neill wrote:

> Self regulation means the right of a baby to live freely, without outside authority in things psychic and somatic. It means that the baby feeds when it is hungry; that it becomes clean only when it wants to; that it is never stormed at nor spanked; that it is always loved and protected.[1]

In another place Neill says,

> I believe that to impose anything by authority is wrong. The child shouldn't do anything until he comes to the opinion — his own opinion — that it should be done.[2]

Finally, in acknowledging the philosophical underpinnings of his concepts, Neill comments,

> Self regulation implies a belief in the goodness of human nature; a belief that there is not, and never was, original sin.[3]

Other concepts grew out of this new movement. The parent was not to be responsible for shaping his child's behavior. The child was not to be forced to carry out household duties nor to obey externally originated standards. Instead, the parent was to be ready if the child came for guidance and to use reason and discussion as his tools.

---

[1] A. S. Neill, *Summerhill: A Radical Approach to Child Rearing* (New York: Hart Publishing Company, 1960), p. 105.
[2] *Ibid.*, p. 114.
[3] *Ibid.*, p. 104.

The influence of this new movement spread quickly. Innovative educators soon began implementing educational procedures based on this new philosophy. Classes for the gifted, retarded, and emotionally handicapped arose partially because of this new "democratic" emphasis. Ungraded classrooms also grew from this movement. All these developments had a positive side; they stressed that each child had the right to progress at his own speed. But the movement didn't stop there. The revolution spread to our courts and penal institutions. It joined with other influences in leading to abolition of the death penalty and the lessening of criminal offenses.

At home, parents were taught that physical discipline could warp their children's personalities. So parents developed a kind of national guilt. Every time they raised a rod or razor strap they wondered if they were somehow inflicting lasting damage to the psyches of their precious children. Many parents gave in to the new movement. In part because of their own reaction to past authoritarianism and in part out of a sincere desire to do the right thing, they were led into a permissive attitude. This has finally culminated in the rebellion, impulsiveness, and lack of respect for discipline and authority so apparent in the culture of today.

In spite of its excesses, the permissive attitude held some vital truth. It recognized the weaknesses of the "children should be seen and not heard" school. Under this attitude children had often been squelched, ignored, punished unnecessarily, and made to feel inferior and unimportant. The permissive movement was trying hard to return a lost sense of dignity and worth to children. This attitude was commendable. But as often happens, the leaders of this movement swung to the opposite extreme. In stressing the fact that children are of value, they ended up saying children are essentially good. In pointing out how authoritarian parents had robbed children of opportunities for self-direction, the permissive proponents taught that children have a potential capacity for *complete* self-direction. And in attacking the abuses of parental punishment, they left the impression all discipline is wrong.

These extreme ideas accord neither with the common sense experience of most parents nor with the teachings of the Bible. They fail at several points. First of all, *they ignore or under-*

estimate the sin and rebellion problem. The Bible teaches that every person born into the world has a bent for sinning and rebellion. Consider the following Scriptures:

> Behold, I was shapen in iniquity, and in sin did my mother conceive me. (Ps. 51:5)
> The wicked are estranged from the womb: they go astray as soon as they be born, speaking lies. (Ps. 58:3)

Any view of child rearing that ignores this basic element of human nature is doomed to failure. Children do not just naturally develop positive attitudes to life. They must have training and correction as well as the new birth to overcome this sin principle.

Second, *a permissive attitude fails to teach respect for authority.* We live in an ordered universe. God has established lines of authority to promote the effective functioning of society. Children are to respect their parents and follow their directions (Col. 3:20, Eph. 6:1-3). Wives are to follow the leadership of husbands (Eph. 5:24). And all of us are to follow the authority of civil leaders (Rom. 13:1).

Our ultimate authority, of course, is God. We are taught to respect God (Ps. 111:10) and to follow His leadership (Prov. 3:5, 6). If children fail to gain a respect for and trust in parental authority, they may later have difficulty submitting to the directions of God and other authority figures. Over-permissive discipline robs children of this essential lesson.

A third failure of the permissive home atmosphere is psychological in nature. *A lack of parental discipline may breed serious feelings of insecurity.* Children have strong feelings and impulsive wishes. While they seek to extend their boundaries and reach their unknown limits, they also become anxious and insecure when no limits are available. Can you imagine being placed in a strange world as a young child and being told, "You may go where you want and do anything at all you want to do"? Almost immediately you want to ask, "But how far can I go?" "What is it safe to do and not to do?" "What activities might be dangerous?" Or, "Isn't there someone here to help?" Without some parental discipline, children are left at the mercy of their own impulses and childish wishes. This can be a frightening experience.

THE AUTHORITARIAN PARENT

History is filled with interesting phenomena and lessons. One of these is the repeated tendency to swing from one extreme to the other. A period of restraint and control is followed by a time of rebellion and revolt. A time of peace is followed by a time of war. A dictatorship is rejected for democracy. And the abuse of women is replaced with women's liberation. Nowhere is this more true than in the parent-child relationship. We are continually swinging from a strong, authoritarian control to a permissive, child-centered environment. Then, after a period of chaos and freedom, we swing back to the controlling mode.

The opposite of the permissive parent is the authoritarian one. In contrast to the permissive parent, this ones sees children needing large amounts of adult control. He uses power as his major weapon. Since he knows he is bigger and stronger, he tries to win obedience out of strength. To some this seems to accord more with the biblical view of man; it teaches that children are rebellious and in need of outer control. Because of this, Christian parents have often been duped into an authoritarian approach to child training. They use large doses of physical discipline and refuse to discuss decisions calmly with their children. Parental standards are supposed to be followed "because I said so!" Any challenge to the parents' authoritative role is strongly resented. During the last few years many people, including a large number of Christians, have begun to reemphasize strongly the need for parental authority and power. While this movement is an understandable reaction against the permissiveness of our society, it is apt to return us to the same authoritarian excesses that originally called forth the permissive movement. Consider the following quotation from a Christian author.

> In my opinion, spankings should be reserved for the moment a child (age ten or less) expresses a defiant "I will not!" or "You shut up!" When a youngster tries this kind of stiff-necked rebellion, you had better take it out of him, and pain is a marvelous purifier. When nose-to-nose confrontation occurs between you and your child, it is not the time to have a discussion about the virtues of obedience. It is not the occasion to send him to his room to pout. It is not appropriate to wait until poor, tired old dad comes plodding in from work, just in time to handle the conflicts of the day. You have drawn a line in the dirt, and the child has deliberately flopped his big hairy toe across it. Who is going to win? Who has the most courage? Who is in charge here? If you do not answer these questions conclusively for the child, he will precipitate other battles

designed to ask them again and again. It is the ultimate paradox of childhood that a youngster wants to be controlled, but he insists that his parents earn the right to control him.[4]

This approach reflects neither a biblically sound nor a psychologically healthy attitude toward child rearing. Although defiance should be dealt with, the proper resolution of defiance does not come through a "nose-to-nose confrontation."

Does God draw a line in the soil and threaten to clobber the next person who steps across it to challenge His authority? Does He say He will resolve our "stiff-necked rebellion through a nose-to-nose confrontation using pain as a purifier?" Of course not! There is eternal punishment for those who reject Christ's atonement. And there is discipline for wayward children. But this discipline is not to "show him who's boss." This parental attitude reflects more on the insecurity of the parent and his fear of losing control than it does on the genuine needs of the child. Parents gain respect by a loving and calm exercise of their authority, not by the stubborn application of parental power.

Some parents are looking for a fight. Not understanding the many causes of child behavior, they think children are attacking their authority and being strong and aggressive when they are actually feeling weak and threatened. Anger and apparent stubbornness are usually reflections of a weak-feeling, frightened child or parent. When we feel confident and secure, we have no need to arch our backs and prepare for battle. *What children need at this point is an understanding ear.* Without giving in to unrealistic or inadvisable demands, we should take time to ask our children what they are really feeling. We should allow them to acknowledge their negative emotions without turning on them with our own form of juvenile hostility.

But how, you ask, can we tell if we are authoritarian? When are we abusing our parental prerogatives? Although authoritarian attitudes show themselves in many ways, there are a few good indicators of their presence. *Our own anger and feelings of frustra-*

---

4 James Dobson, *Dare to Discipline* (Wheaton, Illinois: Tyndale House Publishers, 1970), pp. 27-28. Used by permission. This is a very well-written and helpful book. I cite this and another quotation (p. 126) because I believe they reflect an unhealthy authoritarianism rather than a loving biblical authority. Insecure parents may take this kind of comment and use it to reinforce their authoritarian patterns under the guise of Christian training.

tion are the best indicators of the abuse of parental power. The Bible teaches that hostility is sin.[5] Anytime we force children to do something when we're angry we're abusing our power. It is impossible to discipline effectively when we are angry. Responsibility is divinely delegated to parents so they can guide and discipline children out of love, experience and wisdom. It is not delegated to parents so they can force children into conformity when they are angry.

A second indicator of authoritarianism is the attitude "Because I said so" or "because I'm your parent." Do you sometimes interrupt your children's television program or some other activity with

---

[5] For a more complete discussion of the problems associated with parental anger, see chapter eleven of my book *Help! I'm a Parent* (Grand Rapids: Zondervan, 1972).

the excuse, "Since I'm an adult I have the right to interrupt?" If so, you are likely abusing your parental power. How do you feel when someone turns off the television in the middle of a program *you* are watching? Doesn't it make you angry? The same thing happens with our children. Although we may think their programs are unimportant, they aren't to the children. When we interrupt we are telling them, "You are not so important as we are. When you get big, you will be important, too." This is an unfortunate attitude. It degrades children, causes depression and resentment, and interferes with positive moral growth.

A final indicator of the overuse of parental power is our use of spanking and power-oriented forms of discipline. Spanking definitely has a place, but its overuse often represents authoritarian attitudes. When we respect children we find ways of communicating and forms of discipline that are far more effective than spanking. Spanking usually represents our first impulsive reaction to misbehavior rather than our reasoned plan for discipline.

As children are given opportunity to clearly express their viewpoints and their feelings, their stubborn rebellion usually fades. When it does not, we may have to use our power, but even then it should be done calmly and never in frustration or in anger. In chapter seven we will go in depth into the biblical teaching on the use of parental power and authority. Before that, however, let's take a look at another interesting source of insight into children.

STATISTICS TALK TO PARENTS

During the past thirty years psychologists and sociologists have carefully studied the effects of various forms of upbringing upon the development of children. Rather than blindly accepting each new trend or theory, these researchers have tried to study objectively the outcomes of various types of parent-child relationships. These years of research combine to give us many important guidelines for rearing children.

For our present purpose I would like to take one well-done research study and look at it in depth. This research[6] studied the effect of three types of child-rearing practices upon the moral development of 444 school age children. In short, the authors

[6] M. Hoffman and H. Saltzstein, "Discipline and the Child's Moral Development," *Journal of Personality and Social Psychology* 5, No. 1 (1967):45-47.

wanted to answer the question, "What type of parental discipline helps build morality in children?" The reverse side of this question is "What type of parental discipline hinders development of moral values in children?"

Although we all use many types of discipline, most of us rely more heavily on one method than others. Some of us naturally rely heavily on our authority and power-oriented disciplinary techniques. Other parents repeatedly communicate disapproval of their children by criticism or implied rejection. Still other parents find it very natural to discuss things with their children and quietly point out the reasons for choosing certain moral actions.

Since most of us fall largely into one of these categories, the researchers divided parents into three groups on the basis of their most frequent use of power, love withdrawal, or reasoning disciplinary methods. The next section discusses in some detail the way these parents and children were tested to answer the question, "What type of parental discipline most effectivly instills a good morality?" This study will interest you if you have an intellectual curiosity for objective studies. If not, you may want to skip over to the next section where a summary of the results is given.

THE STUDY

The authors divided parents into three categories on the basis of their child-rearing methods. Then they compared the moral development of children from these different groups. The three general categories of disciplinary techniques were designated as either power-oriented, love withdrawal, or induction. The authors define these three general categories of discipline as follows:

(1) *Power assertion:* This category included physical punishment, deprivation of material objects or privileges, direct application of force, or the threat of any of these.

(2) *Love withdrawal:* This category included techniques where the parent to some extent withdrew his love from the child. Examples of this were turning his back on the child, refusing to speak to the child, stating that he disliked the child, or isolating him.

(3) *Induction:* This category included appeals to the child's moral judgment by pointing out the consequences of the child's actions for the parent or other involved person.

After the parents were divided into these three groupings, each child was administered a battery of tests relating to different aspects of morality. These tests were primarily designed to measure

(1) The intensity of guilt experienced following his own transgressions
(2) The use of moral judgments about others which are based on internal rather than external considerations
(3) Whether the child confessed misdeeds
(4) Whether the child accepted responsibility for his misdeeds
(5) The extent to which he showed consideration for others

In other words, the researchers were trying to answer the following questions:

1. What type of parental discipline leads children to develop a guilt feeling after a misbehavior?
2. What type of discipline leads children to make moral evaluations about other children based on mature, internalized values rather than an external considerations?
3. What type of discipline leads children to confess their misdeeds?
4. What kind of discipline leads children to accept responsibility for their misbehavior?
5. What kind of discipline causes children to be considerate of others?

Without going into technical details, let us be aware that the authors developed methods of measuring each of these five areas. For the authors to measure the extent of the children's guilt, for example, each child read a story and was asked to finish it with "what happens afterward." In the first story a child died through the negligence of an older child. In the second story a child cheated in a swimming race and won. The stories were constructed so that the person would very likely not get caught for his misbehavior. After the children wrote their conclusions, the stories were ranked on the intensity of guilt attributed to the main character. At one end of the continuum were those who showed no conscious self-critical actions, while at the other end were stories where the guilty person showed deep remorse, such as suicide.

To test consideration for others, the authors evaluated the chil-

106

dren by sociometric devices which asked them to select those in their classroom they felt would be most sensitive and considerate of others. Similar measures were used to evaluate the degree to which children confessed their misdeeds and accepted responsibility for their own behaviors.

But the evaluation wasn't limited to the children. Parents, too, were studied. The parents' disciplinary methods were evaluated by both the child and his parents. Every child in the study was asked to imagine four specific situations which occasioned parental discipline.

In the first situation the child delayed complying with a parental request. In the second the child was careless and destroyed something of value. In the third situation the child talked back to the parent. And in the fourth the child had not done well in school. For each situation there was a list of from ten to fourteen possible parental disciplinary practices. The children selected the practices most frequently used by their parents. Each of these disciplinary practices belonged to one of the three categories — power assertion, love withdrawal, or induction.

The same list of disciplinary settings was also given to the parents. They rated themselves on the frequency of different forms of discipline, to balance their perspectives with their children's.

RESULTS

The findings of this study are rather dramatic. In *every* type of morality measure, the group of children whose parents used disciplinary methods that largely involved reasoning and pointing out the consequences of behavior (inductive) had higher moral development than the other two groups. On the other hand, in four out of the five measured areas of morality, the group of children whose parents made much use of disciplinary techniques involving force (power-oriented) had inferior moral development.

In other words, there is an order of effectiveness of disciplinary techniques in developing morality. The least effective methods are power-oriented. These include spanking, force, removal of privileges, and the threat of these and similar measures. The more these disciplinary techniques are used, the poorer the moral development of children will be. Subtle and obvious withdrawal of love also turns out to be an inadequate method of instilling moral values.

By far, the most effective disciplinary methods are those using reason. By discussing the negative consequences of behavior, children are best helped to develop a mature morality. If we want to help our children develop a healthy sense of conscience and moral judgment, we should communicate lovingly and utilize disciplinary methods that discuss the consequences of improper behavior rather than utilizing physical power to punish or coerce children into good behavior.

POWER FAILURE

But why is it that parental power is largely ineffective in instilling moral virtues? We all know that a swift kick in the pants can alter misbehavior. And we also know that a hard spanking may encourage a child to shape up. In fact, the Bible says there is a place for physical discipline. Proverbs 13:24 says, "He that spareth his rod hateth his son: but he that loveth him chasteneth him betimes [early]." In a similar vein Proverbs 19:18 reads, "Chasten thy son while there is hope, and let not thy soul spare for his crying." If the Bible recommends physical discipline, why do psychological research and experience indicate its ineffectiveness? To understand this apparent conflict, we need to look at the moral implications of the various methods of discipline. The basic attitude underlying all types of mature morality is love. The Bible says the whole law is fulfilled in one commandment... "Thou shalt love thy neighbour as thyself" (Gal. 5:14). In other words, moral training boils down to helping our children develop a love and respect for God and people which will result in appropriate moral choices. All of the first four stages of morality are preparatory to this goal. They should be used as little as necessary to control children as they are growing toward the mature love ethic of level five.

Which type of discipline promotes the development of this love ethic most effectively? What is the result of the frequent use of parental power? It may force desirable behavior, but it certainly doesn't foster love and concern for others. Instead, parental power actually reminds children of their weak and inferior position. It fixes them at the fear motivation of level two. By doing this, and

108

by communicating our own frustrations, we actually generate more hostility and frustration. This anger is diametrically opposed to love for others, the core attitude of mature morality.

But there is another drawback to parental power. In power-assertive methods the primary lesson is "Do what is expected or you will be punished." This is a self-protective, self-centered type of morality. It causes children to behave to avoid punishment rather than to avoid hurting others. By contrast, inductive discipline based on good communication teaches "Do what is expected so that others will not be harmed." This is a mature morality. It involves a healthy empathy and corresponds to the fifth stage of moral development discussed in chapter five.

One final word should be said about parental power. Both the Bible and psychological research indicate there is a place for the exercise of parental authority. The problem is that some of us tend to overuse our authority to squelch our children, relieve our own frustrations, or protect our threatened self-esteem. When physical discipline and power are used selectively with good-sized doses of open communication and accepting attitudes, they play an important role in discipline, especially during the first five or six years of a child's life.

Let's summarize the effects of the permissive and authoritarian approaches to child rearing. The lax discipline of permissive parents often leads to impulsive, self-centered personalities. Although children reared in this atmosphere may be spontaneous, free, and flexible, they are apt to be lacking in self-discipline, concern for others, and respect for authority. This attitude inhibits a mature morality.

At the other extreme, power-oriented, authoritarian home atmospheres tend to breed one of two personality types. Children of these families either submit to the strong authority and become conforming, dependent personalities or turn against the parental authority in anger and rebellion. The power-oriented, authoritarian parent actually inhibits moral growth by his overuse of restraint and fear motivations. Children are forced either to give in passively at the cost of losing their independent identity and spontaneous self-expression or to rebel against their parents' values in an attempt to find this sense of personal individuality.

109

APPLICATION

Chapter six discusses two models of child rearing that lead to inadequate moral development. These exercises are designed to help clarify the problems caused by parental permissiveness or authoritarianism.

EXERCISE I

With your mate or another parent, have a mock discussion of the pros and cons of permissiveness.

A. Begin by advocating parental permissiveness and trying your best to convince your discussant of the virtues of permissiveness. You may even see if you can find Scriptures that seem to support your views. List all the advantages of permissiveness you can think of.

1. ....

2. ....

3. ....

4. ....

5. ....

B. Now take the other side of the argument. What problems do

110

you see with permissiveness? How can you support your points
of view?

1. ....

2. ....

3. ....

4. ....

5. ....

EXERCISE II

Arrange another discussion on the merits of authoritarianism.

A. Begin by listing all the reasons for an authoritarian home and
the frequent use of parental power.

1. ....

2. ....

3. ....

4. ....

5. ....

B. Now list all the disadvantages of authoritarianism you can
think of.

1. ....

2. ....

3. ....

4. ....

5. . . . .

EXERCISE III

All parents are on a continuum from extreme permissiveness, characterized by few or no parental controls and complete freedom for the child to choose his goals and actions, to a strong authoritarianism that makes heavy use of spanking, physical control, parental power, and the "children should be seen and not heard" attitude. In the middle is a balanced parental authority that gives children guidance and discipline but respects their sense of worth and leaves plenty of room for self-determination and responsibility.

A. Complete the following ratings:

1. Rank yourself on the following scale.

1	2	3	4	5
Strongly Permissive	Mildly Permissive	Reasoned Democracy or Sensitive Authority	Mildly Authoritarian	Strongly Authoritarian

2. Have your mate or a friend rate you.

1	2	3	4	5
Strongly Permissive	Mildly Permissive	Reasoned Democracy or Sensitive Authority	Mildly Authoritarian	Strongly Authoritarian

3. If you have teenagers, have them rate you.

1	2	3	4	5
Strongly Permissive	Mildly Permissive	Reasoned Democracy or Sensitive Authority	Mildly Authoritarian	Strongly Authoritarian

B. What attitudes or behaviors led you to rank yourself as you did?

. . . .

. . . .

C. Discuss your ratings with your mate and your teenagers. What

did you learn from that discussion? . . . .

112

. . . .

. . . .

. . . .

D. Rank each of your parents on the same scale.

1	2	3	4	5
Strongly Permissive	Mildly Permissive	Reasoned Democracy or Sensitive Authority	Mildly Authoritarian	Strongly Authoritarian

1	2	3	4	5
Strongly Permissive	Mildly Permissive	Reasoned Democracy or Sensitive Authority	Mildly Authoritarian	Strongly Authoritarian

E. How do you account for the similarities and differences between your attitudes and disciplinary procedures and those of your parents?

. . . .

. . . .

. . . .

. . . .

EXERCISE IV

A. Take one recent time when you used your parental power and an authoritarian attitude to try to guide one of your children.

1. What was the attitude or behavior you wanted your child

to adopt? . . . .

. . . .

. . . .

. . . .

2. Describe your communication or disciplinary procedure.

. . . .

. . . .

. . . .

3. Did you get the behavior you wanted? . . . .

. . . .

4. What attitude or emotions (either expressed or hidden) do you think your child developed from the interaction? (Love, respect, fear, resentment, inferiority, etc.) . . . .

. . . .

. . . .

. . . .

5. What level of morality will that kind of attitude lead to?

. . . .

B. Take one recent time when you exhibited a permissive attitude.

1. Describe the situation . . . .

. . . .

. . . .

2. What was your child's attitude or choice of action in this

situation? ....

....

....

....

3. Do you believe your child's reaction to the permissiveness
   warrants the continuation of that attitude? .... If so,
   should there be any limits placed on him at all? ....
   Why? ....

   ....

   ....

C. Describe one recent time when you exercised your parental
   authority but you did it in a loving, positive way.

   1. Describe the situation ....

      ....

      ....

   2. What did you do? ....

      ....

   3. How did you feel as you corrected him or exercised your
      authority? ....

      ....

. . . .

. . . .

4. How did your child react in response to your discipline or authority? (Discuss both his behavior and his attitude.)

. . . .

. . . .

. . . .

CHAPTER SEVEN

PROMOTING MORAL GROWTH

In chapter six we discussed two parental attitudes that inhibit personal and moral growth. We saw that permissiveness and authoritarianism both interfere with our children's growth toward maturity. In this chapter we will consider the positive side of moral training. We want to answer the question, "What can parents do to further their children's moral growth?" In doing this we will draw heavily on God's pattern of training us as His children. We will apply His attitudes and disciplinary techniques to our earthly parent-child relationships.

Several attitudes and experiences are especially important for the development of mature morality. If we successfully provide these essential ingredients we may be sure our children will get off to an excellent start in their moral development.

EMPATHY AND LOVE

At its most basic level, mature morality is based on a loving concern for the welfare of other people. As we saw earlier, conformity based on external restraint, fear of punishment, or an internalized parental threat is really quite inadequate. Underneath these externally correct behaviors are immature and selfish attitudes.

Our first goal in moral training must be to help our children develop their ability to love. This ability comes only as children first experience love from us. Love is a response that is set in motion by our own reception of positive vibrations from God or

117

other people. When someone tells me, "My problem is I just don't love God enough," I usually reply, "No, that's not your problem. Your problem is you don't know how much God loves you. You see, it's impossible to be consciously experiencing the love of God and not love Him in return."

The Apostle John made this clear when he wrote, "Herein is love, not that we loved God, but that he loved us, and sent his Son to be the propitiation [satisfaction] for our sins" (1 John 4:10). Later in the same chapter John said, "We love him, because he first loved us" (1 John 4:19).

Sometimes we reverse this principle. We think, "I ought to love God more." Or, "I should love Him more." We try to conjure up love through some "power of positive thinking." This will never work. Although we may stir up a few temporarily positive feelings or even an abundance of external, seemingly loving actions, this process will soon fail. We are like wells that soon run dry. Unless we are continually being filled (feeling loved) we will run out of things to give. God didn't start by telling us to love Him; He started by creating and by giving. Only after He demonstrated His love beyond question did He ask us to return it. The same is true for us as parents. We will fall flat on our faces if we try to teach morality to our children without a thorough and effective base of love. Before we ask our children to do loving things for other people, they must feel strongly loved themselves.

At this point we need to distinguish between feeling loved and being loved. Every normal parent loves his children. And every child intellectually knows his parents love him. *Unfortunately, this is often not enough.* Even as adults most of us have at some-time wondered if our mate, our children, our friends, or even God really loved us deeply. Although we know in our heads they did, our hearts seemed to say, "They don't." Children feel this even more. Even in the best families children often fail to feel and accept their parents' love. It's not enough to say, "I love you," to our children. We must communicate and do things until our children spontaneously feel, "They love me."

Let's take marriage, for example. We men are sometimes poor at demonstrating affection for our wives. Wives, on the other hand, have a strong need to be shown they're loved in many ways. Sometimes they ask us, "Do you love me?" Since we usually do,

118

we say, "Of course I love you. I married you, didn't I?" Or, "I wouldn't be living with you if I didn't." We fail to sense their inner craving for loving reassurance because we are more oriented to loyalty and providing than we are to the tender emotions of love.

A story is told of two grade school children coming home from school. The older one said to the younger one, "I carried books for her twice and bought her ice cream once. Do you think I ought to kiss her?" The younger one thought a moment and replied, "Naw, I don't think you have to kiss her. I think you've done enough already."

As parents we sometimes have a similar attitude. We think, "Do I have to drop what I'm doing and take time with my children? Don't they know we have done enough already?" But frankly,

we often *haven't* done enough. God didn't say to mankind, "Of course I love." Instead, He sent His Son. Christ didn't say, "Of course I love." He died for us. Sometimes we need to pause and ask ourselves, "Do my children *feel* my love?" Remember, the question is not "Do I love my children?" Instead, it's "Right now are they *feeling* that I love them?" This is the basis of all morality. It's the foundation for all later love and mutual self-respect. When children feel loved by us they will soon be able to reach out to others in a loving way. Until they feel our love and empathy they will be unable to have a deep concern for others. It's like giving a starving man a morsel of food and asking him to give it away — generally, he won't! Only after he has eaten is he emotionally free to pass food on to other starving people.

STANDARDS

Another component of morality is a set of standards. In our day of relativistic morals, this deserves sincere attention. Although love and empathy form the foundation for all morality, the current notion that love is the only important ethic is totally inadequate. Under the guise of love, some have developed a new theology that does away with hell and justice. Under the guise of love, others have founded a "new morality" of sexual permissiveness. And in the conservative church, under the guise of "love for God," we have petty bickering, pride, and jealousy.

Since we all have a strong bent to self-centeredness and deception, we must have some objective criteria to judge our actions. This is one reason God gave a set of biblical injunctions. They serve as a measuring rod to remind us when our actions fall short of perfect love.

In choosing standards for our children we should go first and foremost to the Scriptures. God, in His infinite wisdom, knew just what guidelines we would need. These standards were not set capriciously or one-sidedly. Instead, God carefully set these out as guidelines for our own best interests.

We should be very careful if we decide to go beyond these guides. Too many restrictions breed frustrations and resentment. Some parents have a long list of don'ts for their Christian youth. Although these standards vary from place to place, they generally include smoking, drinking alcoholic beverages, dancing, and at-

120

tending commercial theaters. Among some groups the taboos include the length of hair, the shortness of dress, makeup, earrings, and even horseless carriages! Each of these may have their satanic side. And certainly the overuse of any of these is sin. But because of our own strong emotional reactions, many of us set these as divine absolutes for our children. This is not a growth-producing attitude. Instead, we should restrict our standards largely to those spelled out in Scripture. If God had intended all of us to avoid other specific actions He could have mentioned them in the Scriptures.

If we do add extra-biblical guidelines, we should let our children know why we have these standards. We certainly have the right to tell our children smoking may be bad for their health. And we should definitely teach that drunkenness is sin. But when we overemphasize these things we are asking for rebellion. The Bible mentions pride, gossip, jealousy, and similar attitudes as much more important than these external things. If we focus on the proper inner attitudes, these externals will take care of themselves.

In teaching moral standards we must begin with our own example. As we have seen in earlier chapters, children closely identify, not only with our actions, but also with our ideals and values. It's impossible to teach a moral ethic when we are not abiding by it. Christ set a beautiful example for us as God's children. Even though He was God, He obeyed all the commandments. He didn't say, "I'm Jesus Christ. My father's just a carpenter. Why should I honor him?" Or, "I'm God, it's all right for me to steal or kill since I understand the situation." Christ didn't complain about God's standards, either. He happily lived under them in the full awareness that by keeping them He could have the most enriching life.

Christ also set another good example. He was willing to live life in our shoes and go through the same temptations we face. In Hebrews we are told Christ was tempted "in all points like as we are" and that He is "touched by the *feelings* of our infirmities" (see Heb. 4:15). Similarly, we parents shouldn't act as though we are somehow above temptations, let alone above yielding to them!

Children need realistic examples. They need to see the enjoyable life-style that comes from Christian living. But they also need to see that we are human, too. We should, of course, set a good example. But sometimes we conveniently fail to mention our own weaknesses to our children. We think, "If they know my sins they would lose confidence in me." Or, "If I'm to set a Christian example, they must not know my failures. Oh, of course, I'll tell them I have problems and mention one or two little mistakes, but the really serious ones I'd better hide."

Consider a teenage daughter coming home from a late date. She says to her mother, "Well, Mom, something really happened to me tonight. Bob and I were parked and I really got turned on." Then the mother replies, "I understand that, honey. The same thing happened when I was dating. At times like that it sure is hard to control yourself, isn't it?"

What dedicated Christian mother talks this way to her teenage daughter? Instead, she would more likely say with some facade of personal virtue, "You've got to be careful, honey. Perhaps you shouldn't date him again."

In saying this she is giving her daughter the message that she is somehow bad, weak, and unable to control her feelings as a Christian should. That immediately stops open communication. How much better to be honest and openly discuss this common dating conflict. This is not to say the mother lists off all the boys she has necked with or go through some story of her own adolescent problems. Too much of this is unhealthy, too.

Some parents, of course, did not have serious problems controlling their sexual feelings. They may have had only very ideal dating experiences. If this was true of you, that's great; you will have a great deal to say to your teenagers in a positive vein. But you must be sure to listen carefully to your adolescent's struggles and avoid a preaching or condemning attitude.

The essential thing is this. As parents we should try to live out a high standard of Christian living. At the same time we should recognize our own weaknesses. Our children cannot relate to the perfect parent who acts as though he has successfully fended off every serious temptation. Instead, they respect a parent who is in touch with his own past struggles and who now has the maturity to look back and give an understanding ear and wise counsel to his offspring.

SENSITIVITY TO THE CONSEQUENCES OF BEHAVIOR

A third component of morality is a respect for the consequences

122

of behavior. The essence of morality is that the consequences of our contemplated actions guide our daily decisions. We choose to perform certain deeds because they will have a constructive influence on the lives of others. Similarly, we refrain from other actions because they might do others harm. In the Apostle Paul's day, some new Christians were afraid to eat meat that had been sacrificed to heathen idols. Although Paul knew he could eat those meats with a clear conscience and hearty appetite, he refrained because he didn't want his weaker Christian brothers to be tempted to eat the meat and end up feeling guilty because of their weak consciences (1 Cor. 8:1-13). Paul refrained because of love and because he knew the consequences his actions would have on others.

As we saw in chapter six, strong reliance on power and force as disciplinary measures does not work. We may force children to behave, but this does little to develop an inner sense of empathy or concern. Instead, the study showed, inductive measures (discussion of the consequences of actions) proved more effective in promoting moral development. The importance of that finding is this:

When children misbehave, we usually need to start the disciplinary measures by discussion rather than by the use of parental power. Our children's misbehaviors are often triggered by misunderstandings, boredom, frustrations, or negative attitudes toward parents. As we build open lines of communication we may be surprised at the number of bad attitudes and behaviors that drop by the wayside.

God deals with us this way. Instead of exerting His parental power He reasons with us from the Scriptures and lets us learn from the consequences of our actions. Although He sometimes finds it necessary to intervene and discipline (Heb. 12:5-7), He more often lets us profit from our own behavior.

The parable of the prodigal son is a good example. The father in this story represents God the Father. The son is any wayward child of God.

> And he said, A certain man had two sons: and the younger of them said to his father, Father, give me the portion of goods that falleth to me. And he divided unto them his living. And not many days after the younger son gathered all together, and took his journey into a far country, and there wasted his substance with riotous living. And when he had spent all,

there arose a mighty famine in that land; and he began to be in want. And he went and joined himself to a citizen of that country; and he sent him into the fields to feed swine. And he would fain have filled his belly with the husks that the swine did eat: and no man gave unto him. And when he came to himself, he said, How many hired servants of my father's have bread enough and to spare, and I perish with hunger! I will arise and go to my father, and will say unto him, Father, I have sinned against heaven, and before thee, and am no more worthy to be called thy son: make me as one of thy hired servants. And he arose, and came to his father. But when he was yet a great way off, his father saw him, and had compassion, and ran, and fell on his neck, and kissed him. And the son said unto him, Father, I have sinned against heaven, and in thy sight, and am no more worthy to be called thy son. But the father said to his servants, Bring forth the best robe, and put it on him; and put a ring on his hand, and shoes on his feet: and bring hither the fatted calf, and kill it; and let us eat, and be merry: for this my son was dead, and is alive again; he was lost, and is found. And they began to be merry.
(Luke 15:11-24)

This boy wanted to leave his father's farm. He decided to ask his dad for his share of the family estate, go to the city, and live it up. Notice the father's reaction. He knew the problems this boy was headed for. He loved his son and wanted to help him avoid serious problems. But he gave him the money!

Why in the world would he do a foolish thing like that? We would probably say, "Of course you can't have the money! You're still wet behind the ears and can't even handle your allowance. Besides that, you'll get into all sorts of sin, and I don't want that to happen. When you grow up, I'll let you have your share. Now go on out to the field and work like your older brother!"

But this father took a different approach. He apparently realized his son would not "grow up" by staying home. Instead, he knew he would learn best from the school of hard knocks. So the father let him go. This must have been a difficult decision. I'm sure the dad was tempted to lecture the son and force him to stay home — but he knew that wouldn't work. He gave him the money, wished him well, and went on with his business.

Armed with his newfound wealth, the son headed for a far country. The further he could get from home, the better. He was fed up with that farm and wanted to lose his identity in a foreign land. He sought out the prostitutes, boozed it up, and soon ran through his father's cash. Having no place to turn, he slopped hogs for a little spending money. Things were so bad he was even tempted to eat the pig's food! Think of it — the son of a wealthy farmer was living like a bum! This was the consequence of his behavior; no lecture in the world would get a point across the way this did. Finally the son wised up. He knew his father's servants were better off than he. So he headed home to ask forgiveness.

Seeing his son walking down the road, his father ran and kissed him. He didn't say, "I told you so," and he didn't "rub it in"! I'm sure he was tempted to lecture his wayward son and extract a promise of better things. But he restrained himself. He knew the boy had learned his lesson. Rejoicing over his son's return, the father honored his return with a banquet. He used no other discipline because he had utilized natural consequences.

This story pictures an ideal father. His love was constant. He didn't degrade his son. And he let the boy learn some vital lessons from his misbehavior. Most of all, the boy probably learned a deeper appreciation for his father. This is one of the stepping stones to mature morality. Spanking and other parental interventions work for a while. But when we experience the consequences of our behavior we rarely forget the lesson. We are not learning from someone else's knowledge; we are finding out firsthand.

RESPECT FOR AUTHORITY

Another crucial element of mature morality is respect for authority. All societies require order to endure. The cornerstones of that order lie in respect for the authority of those in places of leadership. Without this respect, society would turn to chaos. One of our major goals should be to teach our children to respect us, God, and other authority figures. The Bible clearly teaches that we should respect the authority of God as well as that of parents and worldly powers (Rom. 13:1; Eph. 6:1; 1 Pet. 2:13-15). But what do we mean by respect? Does respect mean we obey or listen to someone because we fear him? Or does it mean we respect his knowledge and his guidance? An answer to this question is essential for effective moral training.

The Bible has two meanings for the word "fear." *In some cases fear means a form of anxiety, a harmful emotion. At other times it is used in a positive way to mean respect.* In the following passages, "fear" is used to mean a reverential trust in God:

The *fear of the Lord* is the beginning of wisdom: and the knowledge of the holy is understanding.   (Prov. 9:10)

The *fear of the Lord* tendeth to life: and he that hath it shall abide satisfied; he shall not be visited with evil. (Prov. 19:23)

In other passages, such as 1 John 4:18 and those applying to the non-Christian's fear of God, there is a connotation of anxiety and fearfulness.[1] *The Christian is to have a reverential trust in God, but he should never be afraid of the Lord!*

Likewise, a child should trust and respect his parents. But he should never fear them! In discussing the necessity of teaching children respect, a Christian author writes:

My own mother had an unusual understanding of good disciplinary procedures. She was very tolerant of my childishness, and I found her reasonable on most issues. If I was late coming home from school, I culd just explain what had caused the delay, and that was the end of the matter. If I didn't get my work done, we could sit down and come to some kind of agreement for future action. But there was one matter on which she was absolutely rigid: she did not tolerate 'sassiness.' She knew that backtalk and 'lip' are the child's most potent weapons of defiance and they must be discouraged. I learned very early that if I was going to launch a flippant attack on her, I had better be standing at least ten or twelve feet away. This distance was necessary to avoid being hit with whatever she could get in her hands. On one occasion she cracked me with a shoe; at other times she used a handy belt. The day I learned the importance of staying out of reach shines like a neon light in my mind. I made the costly mistake of 'sassing' her when I was about four feet away. She wheeled around to grab something with which to hit me, and her hand landed on a girdle. She drew back and swung that abominable garment in my direction, and I can still hear it whistling through the air. The intended blow caught me across the chest, followed by a multitude of straps and buckles, wrapping themselves around my mid-section. She gave me an entire thrashing with

---

[1] 1 John 4:18, "There is no fear in love; but perfect love casteth out fear: because fear hath torment. He that feareth is not made perfect in love."

Hebrews 10:31, "It is a fearful thing to fall into the hands of the living God."

Romans 8:15, "For ye have not received the spirit of bondage again to fear; but ye have received the Spirit of adoption, whereby we cry, Abba, Father."

2 Timothy 1:7, "For God hath not given us the spirit of fear; but of power, and love, and of a sound mind."

one massive blow! From that day forward, I cautiously re-treated a few steps before popping off.[2]

Is this respect or is it fear? The author acknowledges that he continued to "pop off"; he merely made sure he retreated a few steps until he reached a safe distance. This is fear motivation. Although the incident is humorous, it illustrates a grossly ineffective attempt at discipline. The negative behavior didn't stop. How much better if some calm communication or thoughtful discipline had been applied. Then, perhaps, the son would have sufficient genuine respect that he would not have had to "pop off" any longer!

Some insecure parents exert their power by severely punishing a child. They think they are teaching obedience and respect, but they are actually instilling a negative, neurotic fear. When we punish children in anger, we promote this negative fear and erect barriers between ourselves and our children. Even though they obey, they find it difficult to communicate freely because of fear.

Children need to respect their parents. But respect must be earned through respectful living. It cannot be "won" through power! A child may learn that he can't "sass" his parents without being attacked in return. So he stops sassing or retreats a few feet before making his remarks. But what has been accomplished? The child fears his parents' power but inwardly has even less respect. How can he respect an adult who is angered by a childish attack on his self-esteem? He really can't. The way to win respect is to hear your child out. If he is upset, let him tell you. If you allow expression of his true feelings, you are showing him respect. When you respect your child, he in time returns the favor by modeling your example.

This doesn't mean we allow unbridled verbal or physical expression. There are times when all persons, including children, must restrain their feelings. But in an intimate parent-child relationship, there should be complete freedom to express negative emotions verbally. If a child's language is crude, you may suggest a better way of self-expression. One of the most disrespectful things we can do is say in anger, "Don't talk to me that way!" Or, "You can't feel that way in here." Instead, we should say some-

---

[2] James Dobson, *Dare to Discipline* (Wheaton, Illinois: Tyndale House Publishers, 1970), p. 30. Used by permission.

thing like, "I'm sorry you feel that way. Is there something I can do to help?" If we take this approach we will really earn respect. After we have tried to help we may then need to go on and say, "I respect your right to feel the way you do, but the way you voiced your anger was really not polite. In the future I'd like you to find a better way to express your feelings."

MEANINGFUL WORLD VIEW

So far we have talked largely about aspects of morality that are common to all people. Everyone can develop an emphatic feeling for others. Everyone can learn to accept a set of standards. Everyone can learn to respect the negative consequences of misbehavior. And everyone can learn to respect authority.

At this point a new dynamic may enter the picture. If our children are to have a deep sense of moral values, they must learn to see life from God's eternal perspective. Many decisions, commandments, and experiences in life take on new meaning when seen in terms of this Christian world view. Why should children obey their parents, for example? Why should a Christian couple work to save their shaky marriage? Or why shouldn't a Christian woman become an advocate of radical forms of women's lib?

There are, of course, some very obvious answers to these questions. In each case, the people involved have the potential to be happier and more fulfilled by following their Creator's pattern. But other answers also are important. God has some specific plans behind His counsel. In obeying his parents, a child learns obedience to God and other authorities. In building an enjoyable and lasting marriage relationship, two people illustrate the eternal bond of closeness between Christ and the Church. And in taking her exalted position as a helper to her husband, a wife portrays the divine truth of our exalted position as submissive sons of Christ.

A Christian world view also helps to free us from the press of momentary impulses. As we realize God's great plan for the ages and our future life in heaven, we become better able to postpone some immediate earthly pleasures for a life of meaningful service to Christ.

A divine perspective of life also helps explain the necessity for divine absolutes. We all tend to overestimate our objectivity and reasoning abilities. None of us goes through life without repeatedly thinking we know better than God how to run our lives. Sometimes this shows itself in our refusing to accept a call to full-time Christian work. Sometimes it shows itself in our wanting to take revenge on those we feel have wronged us. And sometimes it shows itself through our subtle rejection of biblical teachings on how to live our lives.

Children also need to become fully aware of the universal human tendency to live life independently of God. By helping our children understand Adam and Eve's initial rebellion (Gen. 3:1-19), the inherent nature of sin in each of us (Pss. 51:5; 58:3; Rom. 5:12; Eph. 2:3), and the personal sins we all commit (Rom. 3:10, 23) we help our children see the need for biblical absolutes as well as moment by moment dependence on the Holy Spirit. We need biblical absolutes as a check on our human reasonings.

We don't do this to make our children feel inferior and inadequate to make decisions on their own. Instead, we want to help them understand the necessity of checking their decisions against the unchanging truths of the Word of God. Sensitivity to our sinfulness and rebellious nature must then be balanced with a sense of confidence and personal individuality. That ingredient of morality will be discussed later in this chapter.

SALVATION AND THE INDWELLING HOLY SPIRIT

A general Christian world view is still not sufficient for effective Christian training. The Bible teaches that we are all estranged from God because of the great gap between His holiness and our sinfulness (Rom. 3:23). Since God is holy, He cannot fellowship with sin. Since He is just, He must punish sinners. But since He is love, He paid the penalty for our sin to remove our punishment and allow us to fellowship freely with Him.

When we accept Christ as personal Savior, we immediately gain the resource for a new viewpoint on life. There is a whole realm of spiritual truth and understanding that opens up to us. 1 Corinthians 2:14 says:

> But the natural man receiveth not the things of the Spirit of God: for they are foolishness unto him: neither can he know them, because they are spiritually discerned.

When we lead our children to a saving knowledge of Jesus Christ, we are not just settling their eternal destiny. We are also leading them to a daily resource for a meaningful life experience and a truly mature morality. The Holy Spirit living in our children will lovingly correct them in our absence and gradually bring experiences to their lives that will encourage both a deep spiritual commitment and a lasting moral life (John 14:26; 16:12-15; 1 Cor. 12:8).

PERSONAL IDENTITY AND A SENSE OF INDIVIDUALITY

Until our children have left our homes and our direct parental influences, they cannot be completely responsible for their own behavior. As long as they are under our roofs there is a certain moral irresponsibility. Whether we consciously try to avoid it or not, we do have many subtle influences on our children.

From birth onward, our goal should be to free our children from our control and prepare them to accept responsibility for their own decisions. To do this is no simple matter. We all want to control our children. We love them and we want them to avoid potentially damaging experiences. This is normal. In fact, we are specifically instructed to train up our children properly (Eph. 6:4). But we also often tend to overprotect our children and keep them dependent longer than we need. We make decisions they could make themselves. We give them answers rather than encouraging them to seek their own information. And we try to instill a guilt-and-fear-based motivation to insure their loyalty to our standards even when we're gone. All of these rob children of responsibility.

As our children gradually mature, we can encourage them to take on more responsibility. We can allow them to make more choices concerning their dress, their friends, and their activities. As we are sensitive to their capabilities, our role gradually changes from protector and director to guide and friend. By late adolescence our role should have become largely that of example and friend. Hopefully, we will also be their welcome counselor or experienced guide. Our parental functions of protection and discipline should have vanished along with the immature morality of levels one, two and three.

THE CORRECTIVE SELF

In chapter four we discussed the concept of the ideal self. We pointed out that children gradually internalize the goals and standards of their parents and other important people. This ideal

130

self becomes a central motivating force in life. We either try hard to live up to this ideal or turn in rebellion to opposite objectives.

We also saw that children internalize their parents' disciplinary attitudes. If parents shame children into good behavior, the children internalize these attitudes and later condemn themselves for misbehaviors. Although this may lead to improved behavior, it also tends to create depression and lowered self-esteem. When we become angry with our children's misbehavior and subtly reject them, they internalize these attitudes. Later in life when they sin they will feel, "God (or other people) must be angry with me. They don't like me when I act this way." Although this, too, may lead to conformity, it does so out of the threat of rejection and hostile disapproval. This causes neurotic feelings of insecurity, worry, and anxiety. The Bible calls these inner attitudes sinful in themselves.

The above attitudes reflect some of the unhealthy forms of motivation we can use on children. When children live with these attitudes, they gradually accept them as their own and crystallize them into their corrective selves. When they want to improve their behavior, they talk to themselves like this: "I am bad. I'd better shape up or I'll be punished. God doesn't like me this way. I guess I'll try harder." This sort of reasoning is not good. It causes a poor self-esteem and leads to unnecessary anxiety and depression. These attitudes are also harmful and fall short of the fulfilled life God intends for His children.

Let's contrast this type of internalized corrective self with God's methods of leading us to personal maturity. He begins by convincing us of His love. He not only tells us of it; He has demonstrated it repeatedly through His faithfulness to Israel and supremely through the gift of His son.[3]

Second, God sets high standards for us. He calls us to be perfect and holy.[4] At the same time, His attitude is realistic. He lets us know that we will all fall short[5] and that this ideal is reached only

---

[3] John 3:16, "For God so loved the world, that he gave his only begotten Son, that whosoever believeth in him should not perish, but have everlasting life."
[4] 1 Thessalonians 4:7, "For God hath not called us unto uncleanness, but unto holiness."
[5] 1 John 1:8, "If we say that we have no sin, we deceive ourselves, and the truth is not in us."

through a long growth process.[6] In other words, God gives us a high ideal self, but tells us not to be hard on ourselves when we fall short.

God lets us know that He understands our frustrations,[7] loves us just the same,[8] and expects us to continue growing.[9] Rather than always intervening and forcing us to conform, He instructs us in behavior that will help us grow[10] and lets us profit from our own mistakes.[11] In other words, God says to His sinning children, "That attitude or action is harmful to yourself or others. Christ died to pay the penalty for it and break the power of sin. You are important to me, and I want to help you grow because I love you. Here are some suggestions that can help."

When He must discipline us, He always does it out of love. In discussing sinning Christians, John writes, "My little children, these things write I unto you, that ye sin not. And if any man sin, we have an advocate with the Father, Jesus Christ the righteous" (1 John 2:1). The author of Hebrews writes, "For whom the Lord loveth he chasteneth, and scourgeth every son whom he receiveth. If ye endure chastening, God dealeth with you as with sons; for what son is he whom the father chasteneth not?" (Heb. 12:6, 7).

God is neither a permissive parent nor an authoritarian one. Similarly, the Christian family should not be based on either of these models. Instead, the Christian parent should combine the attributes of a loving authority (God's parental role with us) and a reasoned democracy (necessary because we do not have all of God's divine attributes of omniscience).

The Christian family should recognize that God has delegated

---

[6] Philippians 3:12, "Not as though I had already attained, either were already perfect: but I follow after, if that I may apprehend that for which also I am apprehended of Christ Jesus."

[7] Hebrews 4:15, "For we have not an high priest which cannot be touched with the feeling of our infirmities; but was in all points tempted like as we are, yet without sin."

[8] Romans 5:8, "But God commendeth his love toward us, in that, while we were yet sinners, Christ died for us."

[9] Ephesians 4:13, "Till we all come in the unity of the faith, and of the knowledge of the Son of God, unto a perfect man, unto the measure of the stature of the fulness of Christ."

[10] 2 Timothy 3:16, 17, "All scripture is given by inspiration of God, and is profitable for doctrine, for reproof, for correction, for instruction in righteousness: that the man of God may be perfect, throughly furnished unto all good works."

[11] Galatians 6:7, "Be not deceived; God is not mocked: for whatsoever a man soweth, that shall he also reap."

132

certain roles and responsibilities to the parents (Prov. 22:6). Parents should exercise their authority in the continued awareness that this authority represents a trust from God and is not to be used to bolster their own egos, perpetuate their personal prejudices, or build little empires. Instead, they are to exercise that God-given authority lovingly,[12] consistently,[13] beneficially[14] and with an awareness of their own human frailties.[15]

In ordaining this family structure, God has one goal in mind. He is trying to get us beyond the power-oriented fear and guilt motives to mature morality. He is amazingly tolerant of our failures and shows an amazing amount of confidence in the ability of the reborn Christian to reach this love-based morality of level five. Under the inspiration of the Holy Spirit, the Apostle Paul wrote, "Whereas the object and purpose of our instruction and charge is love which springs from a pure heart and a good (clear) conscience and sincere (unfeigned) faith" (1 Tim. 1:5, Amplified Bible). Surely this should be our goal with our children.

This is the positive attitude children need to internalize. It sets a high goal but lovingly leads us to this mature morality. We are largely responsible both for the ideals our children learn and for the corrective measures they use on themselves to reach them. If we set *impossible* standards for young children (like always sitting still in church or never listening to rock music), we program them for either inner frustration or outer rebellion. If we *fail* to set standards for our children (like the permissive parent), they will not be motivated to develop their abilities and important personal virtues.

If we set appropriate standards, children will be on their way to maturity. But a very important dynamic enters here. Even when we set realistic Christian standards we may fail. This happens when our disciplinary measures are those of punishment,

---

12 Hebrews 12:6, "For when he punishes you, it proves that he loves you. When he whips you it proves you are really his child" (Living Bible).

13 Hebrews 13:8, "Jesus Christ is the same yesterday, today, and forever" (Living Bible).

14 Hebrews 12:10b, "God's correction is always right and for our best good, that we may share his holiness" (Living Bible).

15 Isaiah 53:6, "All we like sheep have gone astray; we have turned every one to his own way; and the Lord hath laid on him the iniquity of us all."

1 John 1:8, "If we say that we have no sin, we deceive ourselves, and the truth is not in us."

shame, frustration, and rejection. Even small amounts of these attitudes can short-circuit the whole growth process. Unless we help our children grow toward maturity with the healthy disciplinary and corrective attitudes God displays with us, all of our spiritual objectives may go down the drain.

Fortunately, God has not left us without a clear pattern for effective discipline and moral training. As we follow His pattern of parent-child relations we may be sure that our children will develop and maintain a meaningful Christian faith and a high and loving standard of behavior.

APPLICATION

Chapter seven discusses the basic ingredients of mature morality. Although morality and conscience are complex functions, they do have several major components. These are (1) the ability to empathize with others, (2) a set of moral standards, (3) a sensitivity to the consequences of behavior, (4) respect for authority, (5) a meaningful world view, (6) a sensitivity to the leading of the Holy Spirit, (7) a good sense of personal identity and individuality, and (8) a positive attitude of self-correction.

EXERCISE I

A. List two reasons why each of these is essential for mature morality.

1. Ability to love and empathize with others

....

....

2. Set of moral standards

....

....

3. Sensitivity to the consequences of behavior

. . . .

. . . .

4. Respect for authority

. . . .

. . . .

5. Meaningful world view

. . . .

. . . .

6. Sensitivity to the leading of the Holy Spirit

. . . .

. . . .

7. A good sense of personal identity and individuality

. . . .

. . . .

8. A good attitude of self-correction

. . . .

. . . .

EXERCISE II

We have seen that children internalize our attitudes and methods of discipline as their own. As adults they will try to correct themselves with much the same attitude as we the parents evidenced toward them. We also saw that there are two general types of disciplinary attitudes and actions. In chapter four we discussed the internalization of "bad parental attitudes." In chapter seven we have discussed the learning of "good corrective attitudes." These internalized attitudes merge into a general attitude we call the "corrective self."

A. To further an understanding of your child's developing corrective self, complete the items below.

    1. What negative parental attitudes do you think your children are picking up from you?

. . . .

. . . .

. . . .

. . . .

. . . .

    2. Which positive attitudes are they learning?

. . . .

. . . .

. . . .

. . . .

. . . .

    3. To help promote the development of a positive attitude of self-correction, we need to set a good example. List below some attitudes or actions you would like to change in order to further your children's personal growth.

. . . .

···

···

···

···

CHAPTER EIGHT

FIFTEEN GUIDELINES FOR EFFECTIVE CHRISTIAN TRAINING

Throughout this book we have discussed a number of biblical and psychological principles. To help you review and tie together these various insights, this chapter lists and briefly summarizes fifteen important principles from earlier chapters. While memorizing a set of guidelines will not change the behavior of our children, the development of a positive parental attitude based on these insights will do much to move us toward effective Christian training.

1. Remember, your life is the crucial factor in your children's development. Not only will they adopt your physical mannerisms, but they will also incorporate many of your interests, values, and other character traits. Your home life establishes their patterns of reacting to all later authorities. This includes teachers, governmental officials, religious leaders, *and* God. If you are continually in a struggle with your children (consciously or unconsciously), they are very likely to have difficulty submitting themselves to God. Similarly, if they fail to gain respect for you, they will lack respect for others.

2. Experience the reality of Jesus Christ in every area of your life. As your children see you relating God to work and play as well as in formal worship, they develop an appro-

priate concept of the God of the universe who is interested in the affairs of every man.

3. Be creative in your teaching. Spiritual training can easily fall into a rut. Occasionally alter your plan of instruction. See that children participate. And keep the topics to areas of interest to your children. This is especially crucial during teenage years.

4. Keep your goal in mind. We should be guiding (not forcing) our children to the time they can place their own trust in God and learn to make decisions on their own.

5. Minimize power assertive techniques. Although some use of parental power is necessary in early life, the overuse of power robs children of the opportunity of developing mature consciences and leads instead to rebellion or dependency.

6. Teach the consequences of behaviors. When children misbehave, try to quietly reason with them. Point out the harm the behavior causes for others or themselves, and try to find a more positive way of discharging their frustrations or meeting personal needs.

7. Avoid fear motivation. Children should be taught to respect the consequences of misbehavior, but we shouldn't try to use anxiety to motivate behavior. Fear is a negative, inhibiting emotion, while respect of consequences is a helpful concept.

8. Don't teach your children self-condemnation. In trying to motivate children we sometimes try to instill a sense of inner condemnation. We think, "If I can make him feel bad for his misbehavior, he will change." Sometimes by "bad" we mean a sincere feeling of regret at hurting another person. But, at other times, we instill the attitude, "You're a bad person. Aren't you ashamed of yourself." The latter is an unhealthy guilt emotion of self-punishment. While it may lead to behavior change, it also causes feelings of depression and lowered self-esteem.

9. Avoid love withdrawal. Children find it difficult to distinguish between disapproval and loss of love. Our anger and frustration often leave children with the feeling, "They don't love me." We need to be very sensitive to our own

140

reactions to see that our children are clearly feeling our love and acceptance even when we discipline.

10. Help your children develop empathy. An essential ingredient of moral and spiritual maturity is the ability to respond sympathetically to the needs and feelings of other people. Children learn this primarily by living with empathic people. As we can place ourselves in our children's shoes and comprehend their feelings, we are taking the most important step in teaching children empathy. That is demonstrating our concern for them. If we ignore their physical hurts, their childish desires, and the reality of their inner feelings, we are laying the foundation for an unfeeling, self-centered personality.

11. Lead your child to a personal encounter with God. A well-rounded Christian home influence is vital to future spiritual and emotional maturity, but it is not enough. At some point every child must make his own commitment to Jesus Christ. Our basic sinful nature and self-centered desires cannot be educated out of existence by the finest Christian family. They can be merely socialized, of course, but a deep inner problem still remains. By personally asking Jesus Christ into his life as Savior, a child receives a new dynamic. Not only does he receive forgiveness for his sins and the promise of a heavenly eternity, he also receives a new life dynamic, the Holy Spirit.

12. Make time for spiritual instruction. Although we are emphasizing a spontaneous Christian experience that permeates all areas of personal living, we should not minimize the importance of regular biblical instruction. As children enter school age years they can profit greatly by gaining an increasing knowledge of the Bible. This may come through Scripture memorization, family devotions, and Bible stories as well as through Sunday school and church activities.

13. Teach biblical standards. In an attitude of love and understanding, children need to learn what the Bible teaches about personal living. Although the standards are important, they are of little value unless they are taught in the proper way. We must communicate biblical principles in an attitude of love and understanding and by our own example.

141

If we do this, and if we explain the personal applications of biblical standards, our children will come to see their great importance and adopt them as their own.

14. Find the growth potential under every problem. When confronted with childish misbehavior, our first response is usually one of disappointment or frustration. We see the negative results of a childish action or look ahead to future hurtful consequences. This is a necessary parental response. But with this we shouldn't overlook another important truth: behind every problem-misbehavior is a potential growth. We should be grateful for childish misbehaviors. They give us opportunity to instruct children now, before they face the severe consequences of adult behavior.

15. Help your children make their own decisions and encourage them to develop their independent identities and unique capabilities. A major goal of all our moral training should be to lead our children to personal maturity. While we often feel a sense of loss when our children grow up, there is no greater satisfaction for a parent than the realization that his son or daughter has outgrown the need for us as parents and is happily living a stimulating Christian experience of his own.

SUMMARY

As we close this study of our children's spiritual and moral growth, I would like to share one final thought. God has ordained the family unit. He did this both for the benefit of our children and for us. He has chosen us to lovingly guide our children into spiritual and emotional maturity. At the same time He uses them to stimulate our own growth. Their childlike trust, their spontaneous expressions, and their love and admiration give terrific fulfillment to every parent. Their behavior problems and bad attitudes frequently remind us of our needs for growth. These conflicts and problems can be viewed as great personal frustrations or as God-given opportunities for growth.

One of the greatest thrills in life is the opportunity of looking back and seeing how our families have been moving closer to the spiritual ideals God has set for us. As this happens we may be sure that our children will grow to maturity with a deep sense of spiritual commitment and a high sense of moral values.